...efs to Bear is a necessary summons to ... questions of relevance, to be the church ...ed by trauma. We can do this best by reclaiming and then living with humility and generosity practices that we know to be life-giving but have neglected—lament, storytelling, and blessing. The church needs to show up and 'do what we do.'"

BISHOP GREGORY PALMER, resident bishop of the Ohio West Area in the United Methodist Church

"All Our Griefs to Bear is an accessible and practical resource for pastors and other leaders seeking to minister to individuals, families, and congregations who have been affected by the many kinds of trauma that are an ever-increasing reality in our fallen world. In plain language, Joni Sancken describes the types, nature, and effects of trauma and then offers three means of hope and healing with practical examples and suggestions throughout. This is a much-needed and long overdue book!"

ANGIE WARD, general editor of *When the Universe Cracks* and assistant director of the Doctor of Ministry program at Denver Seminary

"This book is a significant contribution to pastoral literature. Psychologically informed by trauma theory, biblically set in lament and reverence for pain, humanly expressed in grieving by way of narrative and story, and with a grasp of the warmth and power of blessing, this book will tug pastoral ministry and congregational life in a direction toward healing. In a time when 'I am blessed' has been reduced to 'How lucky and privileged I am,' Joni Sancken pierces our dark cells of denied or distorted suffering to let in the light of grace and truth."

DAVID AUGSBURGER, professor emeritus of pastoral care and counseling at Fuller Seminary

"All Our Griefs to Bear is a gift to pastors and to churches wondering 'What now?' amidst our collective traumas and griefs. Filled with examples and suggestions to help us acknowledge and honor what we've been through, this insightful, highly practical book will help us confidently begin that essential work. Drawing on her pastoral and trauma-informed expertise, Joni Sancken walks through three communal practices for corporate worship and pastoral care that point us not only to the sustaining hope we have in Christ but also toward the power of that hope to transform our communities—and a world hungry for true healing."

GRACE JI-SUN KIM, professor of theology at Earlham School of Religion, author or editor of twenty-one books, most recently *Invisible*, and host of *Madang* podcast with *Christian Century*

"Seminary professor Joni Sancken has written a timely, practical, and pastoral work on our contemporary experiences of collective trauma and the practices of lament, storytelling, and blessing that can help us process our trauma together. Highly recommended for church leaders, counselors, and all for whom collective trauma is a vivid ministry concern today."

DAVID P. GUSHEE, distinguished university professor of Christian ethics at Mercer University and chair in Christian social ethics at Vrije Universiteit Amsterdam

"Understanding and responding to trauma is one of the most important skills for faith leaders today. As trauma threatens to isolate people, Joni Sancken offers a theologically robust vision for communal resilience that draws people together for healing and wholeness. *All Our Griefs to Bear* relies on sound research in trauma studies, making a complex field accessible through concrete faith practices. This book is an important and timely resource for faith communities and their leaders."

REV. SARAH ANN BIXLER, assistant professor of formation and practical theology and associate dean of the seminary at Eastern Mennonite University

"Joni Sancken is a leader in trauma studies. In these pages, she crafts wise and practical help for rising above the trials many of us face in these difficult times. Her three practices open fresh opportunities to experience anew the redeeming love of God in Christ and to move forward in hope."

PAUL SCOTT WILSON, professor emeritus of homiletics at Emmanuel College, University of Toronto

"With a new and needed lens on the collective impact of the COVID-19 pandemic and its aftermath, *All Our Griefs to Bear* acknowledges the global, personal, and intersectional nature of this shared experience. Joni Sancken's transformative work assures us that 'while long-term unprocessed trauma can be corrosive, our immediate adaptations to life amidst trauma are gifts that help us survive.' This book provides us a place to rest."

ALI W. ROTHROCK, CEO and lead instructor for On the Job and Off and author of *After Trauma*

all our griefs to bear

all our griefs to bear

RESPONDING *with* RESILIENCE
after COLLECTIVE TRAUMA

JONI S. SANCKEN

Harrisonburg, Virginia

Herald Press
PO Box 866, Harrisonburg, Virginia 22803
www.HeraldPress.com

Library of Congress Cataloging-in-Publication Data
Names: Sancken, Joni S., 1976- author.
Title: All our griefs to bear : responding with resilience after collective
    trauma / Joni S. Sancken.
Description: Harrisonburg, Virginia : Herald Press, [2022] | Includes
    bibliographical references.
Identifiers: LCCN 2022026982 (print) | LCCN 2022026983 (ebook) | ISBN
    9781513809755 (paperback) | ISBN 9781513809762 (hardcover) | ISBN
    9781513809779 (ebook)
Subjects: LCSH: Consolation. | Pastoral counseling. | Grief--Religious
    aspects--Christianity. | Resilience (Personality trait)--Religious
    aspects--Christianity. | BISAC: RELIGION / Christian Ministry /
    Counseling & Recovery | RELIGION / Christian Living / Death, Grief,
    Bereavement
Classification: LCC BV4905.3 .S28 2022 (print) | LCC BV4905.3 (ebook) |
    DDC 248.8/66--dc23/eng/20220720
LC record available at https://lccn.loc.gov/2022026982
LC ebook record available at https://lccn.loc.gov/2022026983

Study guides are available for many Herald Press titles at www.HeraldPress.com.

ALL OUR GRIEFS TO BEAR
© 2022 by Herald Press, Harrisonburg, Virginia 22803. 800-245-7894.
    All rights reserved.
Library of Congress Control Number: 2022026982
International Standard Book Number: 978-1-5138-0975-5 (paperback);
    978-1-5138-0976-2 (hardcover); 978-1-5138-0977-9 (ebook)
Printed in United States of America

26 25 24 23 22   10 9 8 7 6 5 4 3 2 1

To my children Maggie and Teddy,

*I'm proud of the ways you are growing in faith,
compassion, resilience, generosity, and peace.
Your hopefulness and joy inspire me.*

I came to explore the wreck.
The words are purposes.
The words are maps.
I came to see the damage that was done
and the treasures that prevail.

—ADRIENNE RICH, "DIVING INTO THE WRECK"

Contents

Foreword

I've recently been in conversation with dozens of pastors and congregations throughout the country. "What's next?" has been our convening question. As we climb out of the pandemic (we hope!) and find ourselves in a changed cultural landscape, we wonder, How are we different from the way we were? What's been lost? Where do we go from here? What must we change in ourselves and our churches?

It's clear from these conversations, with those in church and out, that we are living through a great, disorienting, painful collective trauma. But it's not clear how we are to minister to those who have been buffeted by events of the past few years.

That's why I'm so pleased with Joni Sancken's *All Our Griefs to Bear*. Joni has been called to a ministry of equipping preachers to find the words to help troubled souls. Her earlier book *Words That Heal* showed that she is one of the most interesting preacher/writers in the church today. In *All Our Griefs to Bear*, Joni provides Christians—clergy and lay—the most helpful, healing words we can give ourselves and our friends amid the challenges of our present moment.

Joni has read deeply and widely in the literature of trauma. She looks at trauma through an unashamedly Christian lens and then gives practical application. I'm sure that this book will be of great help to those who care enough to want to say the right thing—in conversations, in counseling, and above all in preaching. Joni's words have certainly helped me have a better sense of how to talk people through their experiences of loss, pain, grief, and disorientation.

Her section on the power of biblical lament is a lively reclamation of an ancient practice for the contemporary church. Drawing on thinkers as diverse as N. T. Wright, Kate Bowler, Charles Taylor, and Luke Powery, Joni offers us so many useful ways to minister to people in their grief, helping people not only bear but also go beyond their pain. Joni has a gift for explication of complex ideas and deep thinking in ways that are engaging and accessible. I'm not surprised. After all, she's a fine preacher of the gospel; she knows how to interest people in subjects that might otherwise intimidate them.

I was particularly struck by the concluding section on blessing, a neglected aspect of the Christian life. Joni shows us how to summon the grace to bless ourselves and others as we go through, are honest about, and by God's grace, even rise above our collective trauma. In all this, this book is a blessing to us all.

Next Sunday I must preach at a little church located at a North Carolina crossroads. The pastor tells me he's fearful that they might not make it much longer, so ravaging has been the pandemic on their membership—two dozen funerals in the last year in a congregation of less than two hundred. Many in their mostly aging congregation are fearful to return to church gatherings. Their few young families are feeling terribly burdened, and Sundays are one of the few days over which they have discretion; they're electing to be elsewhere than church.

When you read *All Our Griefs to Bear*, you'll see why I gave thanks to God for the blessing of Joni's book.

—Will Willimon
Professor of the practice of Christian
ministry at Duke Divinity School

Introduction

It wasn't a special service or unusual Sunday. I didn't know that it would later hold such significance, but February 16, 2020, was my last "normal" sermon. I was serving as a guest preacher at a local Presbyterian church whose pastoral staff had traveled to Israel with a group of congregational leaders. I preached and led worship at the casual and traditional services, shook hands with church members, and sang hymns. My children attended Sunday school and children's choir. I had cookies and coffee in the fellowship hall while my children played with the other kids. A teenaged babysitter had come with us to help shepherd my children; we all rode in the same car.

Two years later, it is strange to recall what feels like a time of innocence. "B.C."—what one of my friend's sons calls the time "before COVID-19" upended our lives. It is hard to find words to describe our experience of today's world. We have lived within a pandemic for over two years, a time which has also been marked by intense racial reckoning, increasing impacts of climate change, and global conflict. Where does one crisis end and another begin? How many experiences can be called "unprecedented" before the word is drained of meaning? More importantly, in this time of collective upheaval and strain, how can we weather the compounding effects of ongoing traumatic stress for our families, our neighbors, and our world? If you're feeling exhausted and overwhelmed, you're not alone.

Trauma refers to circumstances in which one's own life or the life of a loved one is under threat, where one loses a loved one suddenly or unexpectedly, or when the ability to process the experience is exceeded by the magnitude of the experience itself. The global experience of COVID-19 means that everyone in the world has, to some degree, suffered trauma. Individuals, families, congregations, and communities have dealt with this trauma in varying ways and with diverse levels of resilience. Resilience refers to the ability to withstand, adapt, and in a qualified sense bounce back following an experience of trauma.

This book is rooted in practices that can help nurture hope and resilience in congregations and Christian groups. This book may be especially helpful to pastors and laity involved in various leadership roles in the church. The exercises and suggestions may be used by individuals or with groups of varying sizes and can be adapted for diverse contexts and ages of participants. While COVID-19 and associated crises are addressed throughout this book, it may also be useful for engaging other past or future situations of local or broader traumatic stress.

Trauma is a thief. Trauma steals love, physical well-being, hope, and the ability to express, process, or share about one's experience. Precise language is a casualty of the experience of trauma. In her recent book *Atlas of the Heart*, Brené Brown makes a case for greater specificity in the language we use to describe our emotions. The language we use not only helps us process and constructively express emotion, but also shapes our internal experience of emotion.[1] In addition to offering practices that may help process trauma, this book also offers suggestions about how to use language to express what many individuals and groups may be experiencing.

At the time of this writing, a debate unfolding among mental health professionals and trauma researchers concerns how and whether to apply trauma theory broadly to what many have experienced during the COVID-19 pandemic. The broad array of physical, emotional, spiritual, and social responses that many are experiencing look like trauma responses, and experts are tracking increased numbers of people seeking mental health support. Some think that trauma-informed language and approaches to treatment will help normalize what people are experiencing and provide a path for coping, processing, and building resilience. However, others do not correlate the increased demand for mental healthcare with pandemic-related trauma. Well-known trauma researcher Bessel van der Kolk has seen his book *The Body Keeps the Score* experience skyrocketing sales and return to the *New York Times* bestseller list eight years after its publication, but he hesitates to call pandemic-related experiences of pain and intense stress "collective trauma." He emphasizes, "We have to be very precise. Because if we don't know what we are treating, we may give the wrong treatment." He advocates for the creation of new language to describe this moment.[2]

I am not a trauma expert by profession. I am a seminary professor who has read a great deal about trauma and had some training. However, I have seen language and practices oriented toward addressing trauma validate painful experiences and provide tools for processing complex and comprehensive responses. I see value in studying collective trauma and in mining the field of trauma studies as well as theology, scripture, and the rich traditions of Christian practices. With many and varied tools we stand a better chance of moving forward together in ways that bear witness to God's healing, loving, and just intentions for creation.

To that end, chapter 1 of this book explores facets and features of how trauma impacts groups. Studying trauma matters because unattended trauma doesn't just go away. Trauma can adversely affect people and groups physically, socially, spiritually, and mentally. Trauma depletes our physical, emotional, spiritual, and relational capacities and can intensify disconnection and polarization. Trauma impedes connection. Both individually and collectively, we become more likely to experience illness, anguish, and fragmentation.

Ministry in the aftermath of trauma does not seek to forget or somehow move past or "get over" the pain and suffering so many have experienced and continue to experience. However, the promise of the gospel is that we are not sentenced to be forever stuck. The gospel of Jesus Christ promises to liberate creation from that which binds and harms, to save us—even at times from ourselves. This is the greatest treasure the church can offer in the aftermath of intense crises and trauma. God's people are powerfully resilient. The God who has been with God's people throughout history draws especially near and continues with us. Resurrection life is erupting even in the midst of death.

Chapters 2 to 4 of this book focus on specific practices to use in processing trauma: lament, storytelling, and blessing. Each chapter orients readers with theological and biblical background before offering suggestions for using these practices in creative ways to process traumatic stress and nurture resilience, healing, and identity building. These chapters could be used as a foundation for a worship series or could be integrated into other outlets for ministry.

One could easily write many books on each of these practices, and what I offer here is not exhaustive. As practices, lament, storytelling, and blessing are multifaceted and may be contextualized to speak to survivors with a variety of experiences. These actions are rich and laden with meaning. These practices are meant to engage body, mind, and spirit. Because some church communities tend to be less engaged with their bodies, leaders may want to find ways to start slowly and incrementally. My hope is that these practices inspire resilience and creativity, eliciting local ideas and responses that become channels for God's presence and leading.

Therapist Resmaa Menakem writes about the necessity of moving through "clean pain" to clear space to grow.[3] Working through pain is very hard. However, this is the way modeled for us by Jesus, who faced the powers that sought to kill him and end his healing ministry on the cross. As I discuss later in this text, Jesus' own path through this pain clears a space for us to also face our brokenness, sin, and finitude with courage and hope.

This book does not offer a bunch of "shoulds" aimed towards leaders. The truth is that there is much we do not know or understand and cannot predict. This specific global experience of mass trauma is new territory. Many of us have experienced nothing close to this in our lifetimes. Some suggest experiences with similar global reverberations may include World War II[4] or the protracted war in Vietnam, which flooded into homes through the medium of TV. Social media brings a horrific immediacy to trauma experienced around the world. Images and video taken during the war in Ukraine give us front row seats to trauma on the other side of the world.

People were not built to withstand this immense breadth of traumatic stress, and the long-term ramifications are not fully known. However, we can learn from past research on collective trauma and ways the gospel can be honestly and faithfully proclaimed, embodied, and practiced during traumatic crises.

As a Christian living into a journey of sanctification, it has been powerful to be able to continue to work with trauma theory from the angle of collective experience. My deepest prayer is that readers might not only grow in resilience but may also experience a sense of renewed calling. While many traumatic experiences and events are outside of our control, social-systemic brokenness and sin catalyze and deepen trauma for many. This is a time for passionate prayer, lament, truth-telling, forgiveness, compassion for self and others, and action.

The incarnate Christ, wounded and risen, leads the way, drawing us toward each other, creating spaces where we can experience healing, and empowering witness as leaven and salt in a world that has become flattened by pain and bitter on our tongues. May the Holy Spirit spark in all of us a desire not only to engage in healing care in the aftermath of trauma, but also to actively work for a more just and peaceful world. May our beautiful fragility be upheld by God's strength.

ONE

Collective Trauma: A Wound We Share

Our global experience of COVID-19 along with a cascade of associated crises has made the study of collective trauma relevant to all of us. The COVID pandemic is a wound humanity shares, although perspectives and experiences vary widely. In an article in *The Atlantic*, Melissa Fay Greene asks, "How will we remember the pandemic?" She notes that this experience has not been the traumatic "flashbulb" moment of an assassination or terrorist attack; rather, it is a period—still ongoing—in which our individual life memories are embedded.[1] We may ask each other, "When did the pandemic begin for you?"

For me, it began on my birthday, March 12, 2020. In the morning, I enjoyed an indulgent special coffee drink at my local coffee shop with my husband while we asked ourselves if it was really safe to be there. There were only a few of us in the normally bustling space. As the day unfolded, we got news that my daughter's grade school and son's preschool would be closing. My husband decided to close his church.

My seminary classes would also be moving online. We went to a bakery to pick up my cake, the last time our family of four would go into a public space together for more than a year. My husband went to pick up pizza from our favorite restaurant and I sat on the porch swing surveying our neighborhood with a sense of fear and foreboding. New green leaves and daffodils displaying a sense of hope and future growth that I did not share.

Many of us have felt alone and lonely during this season of pandemic and racial reckoning, separated from many places of connection, support, discernment, and meaning. In the United States, individuals have had the burden of making decisions about risk, although because both COVID-19 and racism are community pandemics, our decisions affect others and the actions of others affect us.

At this point, more than two years after shutdowns and intense racial reckoning, *crisis* seems like an understatement to describe our world. The word *trauma* carries some freight. Trauma refers to circumstances in which one's own life or the life of a loved one is under threat, where one loses a loved one suddenly, or when the ability to process the experience is exceeded by the magnitude of the experience itself. Symptoms related to experiences of trauma—digestive changes, bouts of crying, difficulty remembering things and making decisions, elevated blood pressure, and changes in attention span—are the body's way of processing the trauma and dispelling energy created by the flight-fight-freeze response. Trauma responses become especially corrosive when we get stuck. This can happen when our bodies don't fully process the traumatic energy or when trauma is chronic and ongoing.

The global experience of COVID-19 means that everyone in the world to some degree has suffered trauma. Individuals, families, congregations, and communities have dealt with this trauma in varying ways and with diverse levels of resilience. Trauma can cause physical, social, spiritual, and mental harm to people and groups. Trauma siphons away energy and imagination and can deepen polarization and fragmentation. Trauma isolates and makes bodies both individual and collective more susceptible to illness, pain, and brokenness. As we collectively deal with the fallout from the pandemic, political unrest, and social and economic upheaval, the effects of prolonged traumatic stress continue to cascade through our families, communities, and world. Many of us are feeling lost, overwhelmed, and depleted.

This chapter explores aspects and experiences of collective trauma and resilience to help leaders recognize symptoms and behaviors that may be linked to traumatic stress in congregations and other organizations. The following chapters will unpack practices and tools for congregations and individuals to process collective trauma.

CONCEPTUALIZING TRAUMA

You might hear that word, *trauma*, and think, "That doesn't apply to me!" The word *trauma* means "wound" and is primarily used to refer to *involuntary physical stress-related responses* to stressors and events that exceed our individual or communal abilities to process them.

How does trauma feel? The impacts of trauma can sometimes be subtle. What sets traumatic response apart from other responses to situations of extreme stress is the extent of the impact and the sense that a person may be stuck, or mired in the body's response. Signs of trauma may include an inability to sleep or to sleep soundly, brain fog, disconnection between actions and consequences, feelings of isolation, difficulty expressing what is wrong, hypervigilance, feeling out of control of one's emotions, loss of a sense of time, and flashbacks—either emotional or sensory.

Many different types of tragic and harmful experiences, ranging from a one-time event to chronic experiences, can cause traumatic responses. Because traumatic response is housed in bodies—individual and collective—only those who are experiencing traumatic responses can name their experience. Part of the nature of trauma is that we can find it difficult to name or describe.[2]

Along with this more precise clinical way of describing trauma, as a comprehensive response to life-threatening stressors, the term has also taken on a more diffused meaning in our world, leading sociologists to explore how trauma can also function as a broad social concept. Traumatized communities are more than just an assembly of traumatized individuals. As sociologist Kai Erikson puts it, "Traumatic wounds inflicted on individuals can combine to create a mood, an ethos—a group culture almost—that is different from (and more than) the sum of the private wounds that make it up."[3]

Here are some of the sources and indicators of traumatic stress we have recently weathered together, with varying impact on individuals and groups:

- *Historic trauma and intergenerational trauma*, rooted in racism and white supremacy, with effects passing from one generation to the next.
- *Chronic trauma*, as the pandemic and its aftermath drag on for years and as those who have long struggled to make ends meet are now in even greater need because of inflation and other financial instability.

- *Acute trauma,* in our own experiences with illness, sudden deaths of loved ones without our usual means of processing or marking or bearing witness, and political violence and upheaval.
- *Vicarious trauma and compassion fatigue* among all who witness an erosion in the value of human life, suffering, and death—and particularly medical workers and other care providers of all kinds.
- *Collective trauma,* as our life together is irrevocably changed.[4]

These categories are not mutually exclusive. Many experiences of trauma are multicausal and have individual and collective manifestations that can vary over time. Stress-related adaptation is normal. A tragic array of circumstances and traumatic responses are surging through our world. If you're not feeling like yourself, if you feel frozen or immobilized, if you feel keyed up and anxious, if you lack patience, if your emotions are close to the surface, if you're feeling disconnected, if you lack creativity and clarity in your thinking, *you're normal* and your body is, in fact displaying tremendous wisdom. God created our bodies with tools to keep us safe in a crisis.

We will be dealing with the global impact of this event of mass trauma for years after COVID has become endemic.[5] No one would have chosen this path. Yet as much as we long for a return to life as it was—and as much as the media declare it to be so—the truth is that we cannot return to our lives before the cascading crises of global pandemic, racialized violence, political upheaval, and war. We have been changed. While long-term unprocessed trauma can be corrosive, our immediate adaptations to life amidst trauma are gifts that help us survive.

COLLECTIVE TRAUMA: LOSING OUR SENSE OF "WE"

Fractals are unending patterns that are consistent across scale. We see them throughout our created world, from trees to river deltas to broccoli.[6] Fractal wisdom can also help with understanding large-scale trauma. Patterns that we see in individuals that experience trauma are also seen in broader groups.[7] The hopeful news in this observation is that healing that happens for even one person can also generate positive systemic reverberations.

Collective trauma is a wound that we share. Kai Erikson writes, "Sometimes the tissues of community can be damaged in much the same way as the tissues of mind and body."[8]

Erikson defines collective trauma as a kind of wound that is sustained by a society, a "blow to the basic tissues of social life that damages the bonds attaching people together and impairs the prevailing sense of community. The collective trauma works its way slowly and even insidiously into the awareness of those who suffer from it."[9]

Collective trauma dissolves our understanding of shared identity, our "we." This definition resonates with the experiences many have suffered recently because of pandemic, white supremacy, racism, natural disasters, and social unrest. When we cannot see our loved ones, when we cannot gather, when George Floyd's life is squeezed out by the knee of a white police officer, when the Capitol building is stormed by insurgents and elected officials cower, when one million of our fellow citizens die from COVID-19 and these deaths are not collectively marked or grieved, our society sustains a blow. We are all wounded.[10]

Collective trauma has been described as both "centripetal" and "centrifugal"; that is, as a force that both hurls us together and forcefully casts us apart.[11] Communities under extreme stress can become distrustful, brittle, and fragmented as they lose sight of core aspects of identity, experience disconnection from meaningful relationships and practices, and struggle to imagine a future. Conversely, some communities can experience a sense of being pulled together, drawn closer by a shared experience. One thinks of a national and even global sense of "being in this together" after the September 11 terror attacks, or on a smaller scale in support groups for veterans who survived combat, survivors of concentration camps, and support groups for parents who have lost children. These are "clubs" with an extremely high cost of social belonging, clubs no one wants to join, but communities where people have a high level of trust and connection because they share an essentially defining event. Others not immediately impacted may find themselves repelled from those who have experienced this terrible event, illustrating another element of the centrifugal power of trauma.

Stages of collective trauma

While experiences of collective trauma vary, researchers can track distinct stages in how the broad experience of collective trauma unfolds across time (see table 1 on next page).[12] An inventory like this can be personally validating, help name feelings, and offer comfort. We can see how early we are in processing our collective trauma response to COVID-19, how normal our responses are, and that *life will not always feel the way it does right now*.

Loss of trust deepens the pain

The magnitude of mass trauma is often measured by the total number of lives lost.[13] However, feelings of betrayal or lack of trust may have a greater influence on responses. Loss of trust

Table 1. How collective trauma unfolds over time

Stage of collective trauma	Characteristics
1. Event of mass trauma	• Shock • Feelings of being overwhelmed • "Emotional and cognitive turmoil" • "Confusion, and lack of knowledge or clear direction"
2. Immediate aftermath	• Survivors react and respond to specifics around damage assessment • Possibility of protests as part of collective response • Centrifugal and centripetal forces pull people together or drive them apart • Leadership is important • People begin to develop a narrative to help them process the event[1]
3. Months to several years	• Coping • Soul searching • Experience depends on the skills and resources of the community, such as social support and cohesiveness[2] • Some minimize the event; avoid, ignore, or gaslight those who survived the worst[3] • Ignoring the event or related trauma may have short-term collective gains as the majority return to "normal" • Ignoring means that impact for subsequent generations tends to be more pronounced, as the community misses a chance to learn or grow

4. Five to ten years	• Long term effects may appear suddenly or gradually
	• Memories or experiences related to the traumatic event may return unbidden
	• Society is able to engage with the event in a less emotionally charged way
4. Generations	• Evidence of lingering effects in socialization processes
	• Secondary trauma
	• Stress-related health conditions
	• Effects can be traced through families—for example, second and third generations following the Holocaust
5. Centuries	• Future people trace the influence of the event on our understanding of history
	• Scholars note fingerprints of past trauma in present-day beliefs, theology, traditions, art, laws, and stereotypes, and even in neurobiology
	• Collective trauma becomes silent part of the "collective unconscious" that is largely unacknowledged

Source: Peter Felix Kellermann, *Sociodrama and Collective Trauma* (London: Jessica Kingsley Publishers, 2007), 45–50.

1. Narratives can be traced by exploring news footage or headlines in the time following the event. For example, in the weeks and months immediately after the terrorist attacks of September 11, 2001, when George W. Bush's popularity soared, several laws granting the government more authority were passed with bipartisan cooperation that seems shocking today.

2. During the coronavirus pandemic, we have experienced this stage with "the great resignation" as those with the privilege of doing so quit jobs, changed careers, or relocated.

3. For example, after the Vietnam War, both veterans and refugees had an experience of being "avoided, hidden, and rejected."

Table 2. Factors that influence the ability to trust

Predictability	If a community has experienced a particular event before, a second experience may be less traumatic because they are more equipped and less surprised.
	For example, after horrific experiences with a hurricane or earthquake, affected populations often make changes to better survive a future disaster. In the case of a global pandemic and massive societal reckoning around issues of injustice and racism, one could argue that these events have happened before and could have been predicted.
Preventability	If an event is perceived as potentially preventable, traumatic responses are often more pronounced.
	Examples include deadly factory fires caused by unsafe working conditions or fire code violations, the *Titanic* disaster caused by negligence and lack of lifeboats, or a mass shooting where a background check was avoided or the shooter had a history of dangerous behavior. In the case of COVID-19, the rise of the new virus itself was likely not preventable. However, doctors and politicians have asserted that the US government could have acted in more "forceful" or unified ways that could have prevented hundreds of thousands of deaths from COVID-19.[1]

Purpose	If an event of collective trauma was perpetrated on purpose, it may be harder for survivors to come to terms. Examples include genocide carried out by one group against another or targeted attacks against a specific group. Many Americans struggled with the September 11 terrorist attacks because Americans had been targeted. This likely undercut or betrayed an element of American exceptionalism or invincibility that was part of cultural identity.
Periodic duration	The longer the traumatic stress persists, the greater the opportunity for more sustained traumatic responses in a population. When stress is ongoing, responses may become chronic. Examples include racialized trauma, abusive relationships, and those who live in areas of intense conflict or war. As the pandemic and its accompanying impact drags on, we also experience responses related to chronic traumatic stress.

Source: Peter Felix Kellermann, *Sociodrama and Collective Trauma* (London: Jessica Kingsley Publishers, 2007), 37, 43.

1. Allan Smith, "Birx Recalls 'Very Difficult' Call with Trump, Says Hundreds of Thousands of Covid Deaths Were Preventable," NBC News, March 28, 2021, https://www.nbcnews.com/politics/donald-trump/birx-recalls-very-difficult-call-trump-says-hundreds-thousands-covid-n1262283.

is a very common response to a trauma and an experience of broken trust can compound and magnify the pain of the actual traumatic event. Faith in a covenant-keeping God who will never leave us can bring comfort when our basic sense of being able to trust has been rattled.

Trust is baked into our entry and being in the world. Trust is key to attachment in relationships and the ability to develop confidence and independence as a person (or community) grows and matures.[14] Erikson envisions people as "surrounded by layers of trust, spreading out in concentric circles like the ripples in a pond."[15] These bonds help to form our essential sense of "kinship" or "communal belonging."[16] When trauma undercuts this elemental building block, the effects can be devasting. Pastoral therapist and theologian Kate Wiebe puts it succinctly, "Trauma breaks down your sense of trust in yourself, your relationships, and the world."[17] A broken sense of basic trust can make us feel less than human.

Clinical psychologist Peter Kellermann summarizes factors related to one's ability to trust that can influence collective traumatic response with "four P's: predictability, preventability, purpose, and periodic duration" (see table 2, pp. 30–31).[18]

EFFECTS OF COLLECTIVE TRAUMA

Bernice Einstein, a child of Holocaust survivors, vividly describes her experience in her illustrated memoir. Her own experience, a generation removed from the horrors of Auschwitz, has its own color and texture that is both personal and collective. She vividly describes the sensation of being a "Jewish Sisyphus" pushing a boulder of history and memory up an insurmountable hill.[19] She longs to hand this burden back to her parents, but they already carry their own burdens of trauma. She senses her own independence and her privilege of living surrounded by surviving extended family in the safety of Toronto's Kensington Market, but she also feels like an outsider among this close-knit community who bear numbers tattooed on their arms, who relied on each other to make it through a horrific ordeal.

For us, too, the personal and the global experiences of trauma intersect. Naming specific effects, experiences, and feelings are important. Caregivers and leaders can observe the actual effects of traumatic stress on individuals and families in their congregations and communities and help people identify and name what feels broken, hurting, out of sorts.[20]

Pathways of collective trauma

Erikson describes the experience of collective trauma as emerging along two pathways. The first involves "damage to the tissues that hold human groups intact."[21] This means that our sense of connection to each other has been eroded or harmed. The second involves what therapist and theologian Kate Wiebe calls "a shared critical incident" that changes the community through "creation of social climates, communal moods" such that this event and its aftermath dominate the spirit of the group.[22] Both dynamics may often be at work in a community.

Many congregations and church institutions have experienced chronic losses that fall under Erikson's first pathway of collective trauma. In Erikson's words, people have a "gradual realization that the community no longer exists as an effective source of support and that an important part of the [previous group identity] has disappeared. . . . 'We' no longer exist" in the same way with the same sense of "belonging" that we once shared.[23]

Many carry this pain in this season of intense polarization that has generated divisions and split churches, neighbors, friends, and families. In the late fall of 2020, countless American families navigated not only the scourge of COVID, but also divisions related to a close and heated election as they contemplated holiday family gatherings.

Interestingly, groups that experience trauma along Erikson's second pathway, a shared horrific event, can sometimes emerge with a greater sense of community and even a season of growth and creativity.[24] I have witnessed this firsthand. The first congregation I served as a youth pastor and seminary student had been leveled along with much of the surrounding neighborhood by a tornado several decades earlier. This story was a key part of how the congregation introduced themselves to me, showing me a photo album with clippings and pictures and the entry in a local history book. Following the devastating tornado, the congregation's decision to rebuild and recommit to the shattered community spurred a sense of mission and a season of growth.

However, shared traumatic events can also fracture congregations along "fault lines running silently through the structure of the larger community, dividing it into divisive fragments."[25] I saw this firsthand in a congregation where several former students served on the staff. The church was rocked by sexual abuse enacted by more than one trusted leader. As lawyers and local police stepped in to attend to legal matters and criminal charges and denominational officials revoked the credentials of their former pastor, some people left the congregation and others formed opposing camps within the church. Some of these "fault lines" were already present prior to the public revelation of abuse, although having diseased leadership practices that allowed sexual predation to flourish unchecked likely deepened or even caused these fissures much earlier.

Understandably, other members of the leadership team left for their own well-being. My family had moved to another state by the time survivors were sharing their experiences broadly. I experienced heartbreak, outrage, and betrayal reflecting on how I had served alongside these leaders at the school where I formerly taught.

Chronic racialized trauma

Some people and groups experience chronic trauma due to the pain and injury caused by racism, poverty, and financial challenges within both the congregation and surrounding community. Racism creates deep trauma and emotional, spiritual, and often physical harm that can manifest in illness, weakened immune responses, and lower life expectancy.

The concept of "John Henryism" uses the American folktale of John Henry, a Black "steel driving man" who competed against a machine, won, and immediately dropped dead from total depletion as a means of describing how some African Americans feel living and working in a broader context where whiteness dominates.[26] Having brown skin in America means having to work twice as hard and fast. It means living towards a standard of being above all reproach because with brown skin, one already has two strikes against oneself. It means there is no room for error. As "John Henrys" strive against the machine of systemic racism, they may enjoy success, but the constant stress is deadly.

Unrelenting threat and continual pressure inspire unceasing effort to live amidst systemic racism, which contributes to health conditions such as high blood pressure, obesity, and type two diabetes. These appear more frequently in younger Black populations compared to white populations. The COVID-19 pandemic has opportunistically preyed upon those with these same underlying health conditions, killing more than *one out of every seven hundred fifty Black or Indigenous Americans* at the time of this writing.[27] These statistics are staggering.

Cultural trauma

Cultural trauma is related to but has some distinct characteristics from broader collective trauma. Both share the deep pain of betrayal. Anthropologist Clifford Geertz defines culture as systems and symbols or "webs of significance" that we create and reflect upon through interaction.[28] We cannot exist without culture, yet we often may not be aware of culture unless something is terribly wrong and basic trust has been broken. Culture has internal and external expressions, ranging from beliefs, sense of identity, worldview, and that which we value deeply to institutions, rituals, jobs or positions, and physical artifacts. The lens of trauma highlights facets of culture in new ways as members of particular groups and communities experience fallout from the destructive, world-shattering forces of traumatic events.[29]

Cultural trauma unfolds when a community of people who share a linking relationship or distinctive characteristics experience an event or chronic series of events so horrific that it "leaves indelible marks upon their group consciousness, marking their memories forever and changing their future identity in fundamental and irrevocable ways."[30] Maintaining basic trust feels difficult if not impossible.

Using Kellermann's comments on purposeful perpetration of mass trauma, it makes sense that collective trauma that has a strong cultural aspect, such as a particular group being singled out, likely generates more severe stress responses. For example, World War II was a traumatic event on a global scale, but groups singled out for persecution amidst the backdrop of war generally experienced a deeper sense of traumatic response.

Madeleine Albright was nearly sixty years old before she discovered the truth about her family history. Her background was Jewish, and her family had later converted to Christianity before immigrating to the United States. More than two dozen of her family members had died in the Holocaust, including three of her four grandparents. The revelation came as a terrible shock and burden. Albright said she had no idea—not even subconsciously—describing her parents as "remarkable people and I think they did not want to burden me and my siblings with their grief." However, in retrospect, Albright could see the marks of trauma and grief in her parents and how the values they passed along to her grew from their family tragedy. These same values influenced Albright's politics and approach to foreign policy: "The inheritance I received from them includes a commitment to freedom and to human rights."[31]

As trust-destroying and corrosive past and present events interact with a culture, they can destroy important aspects of identity and generate new cultural touchstones. Professor of sociology Mary de Young cites the Irish potato famine as an example of collective trauma that impacted European culture. In a span of four years, almost half the Irish population either died from famine-related causes or emigrated. In addition to horrific personal and family tragedies, the collective toll included decimation of the Gaelic language. Many of the poorest Irish were preliterate, but were caretakers of a rich oral legacy of story, song, and poetry. Those who emigrated or died disproportionately represented Gaelic speakers. Only a few hundred thousand Gaelic speakers remained by the end of the famine, and in the following years, Ireland was rapidly anglicized. A new cultural stereotype developed, linking the Gaelic language with poverty and ignorance. This stereotype deepened the sense of distance between generations of Irish people and earlier aspects of history and culture. As de Young writes, "Cut off from all that is communicated by native language—tradition, identity, and sense of place—post-famine generations left their homeland and sought their dreams abroad, with increasingly profound socioeconomic and political consequences for their native country."[32]

The massive destruction of coastal wildlife following the 1989 Exxon Valdez oil spill opens a window to the painful link between environmental and cultural trauma. While both Indigenous Aleuts and nonnative residents were impacted, Aleuts were more likely to suffer symptoms of post-traumatic stress disorder, as the environmental destruction was more than economic for them. The animals and coastal devastation represented "the crux of Aleut identity, social organization and ideology, and are the symbols through which native culture is transmitted to future generations."[33]

The most devastating circumstances, situations of genocide and systematic or intentional cultural destruction, involve what de Young calls "cultural disintegration." "As Bosnia, Rwanda, Somalia and other places around the world tragically reveal, civil wars, ethnic cleansings, revolutions and mass expulsion and exoduses disarticulate cultural systems and reduce them to meaningless customs, pointless rituals and vague collective memories." In the vacuum of meaningful and rich cultural expressions, "nationalism, tribalism, and fundamentalism" can take root. Human behavior shifts towards distrust, hostility, and negativity rather than positive identity markers.[34]

Past cultural trauma refuses to stay in the past. For many, it is carried forward in deeply physical ways. Resmaa Menakem, writing about the traumas of slavery and racism in the United States, notes that trauma is collective in that it spreads from body to body as well as from generation to generation. Traumatic stress changes our DNA. Even the memory of traumatic stress can be passed down, impacting the development of the yet unborn. Menakem cites studies drawn from working with African American, Jewish, and Native American groups who have experienced extensive historical and cultural trauma.[35] Notably, these same groups also demonstrate remarkable resilience that has helped them survive.

RESILIENCE: RECOVERY, RESISTANCE, AND RECONFIGURATION

Many scholars and clinicians today view *resilience* rather than *return to how things were before* as a more accurate way to frame meaningful life in the aftermath of traumatic stress. Resilience is not a static quality. Responses to traumatic events can vary even within the same person or group depending on the timing and the nature of the traumatic event.[36] Resilience can also be nurtured and developed like a muscle.

Resilience can look very different across individual lives and communities. Researchers have traced at least three types of response: recovery, resistance, and reconfiguration. Using a metaphor of a tree that survives a storm, recovery refers to a tree having been bent over in the storm returning to its natural upright posture; resistance to a tree that stands straight and sturdy in the midst of a storm; and reconfiguration to a tree that permanently changes its shape to accommodate and survive the storm—a change that may allow it to also survive future storms.[37]

Strands of recovery, resistance and reconfiguration can be seen as aspects of resilience in the face of traumatic and life-threatening "storms" of all kinds in our world. The range of resilience responses and the possibility of nurturing resilience are reassuring and validating for us. There is no right or wrong way to do resilience. This is good news!

Recovery

Ash, piles of nails and bolts from burned benches and tables, shattered porcelain cups, a small green drinking fountain, and the burned-out frame of several cars greeted reporter Anna Weiner on a visit to Big Basin Redwoods State Park in late 2020. These are the things that survived. Many redwoods, among the oldest living things on earth, did not. While the pandemics of COVID-19 and racial injustice raged in the late summer and early fall of 2020, some of the largest fires in California history threatened or destroyed acres of precious park land and trees predating the fall of Rome. Weiner had arranged a special tour with ranger Phil Bergman, as the park was not open to visitors.[38] Without landmarks, it was difficult to navigate.

While Weiner's report was understandably marked by disbelief and grief, she also saw unmistakable signs of new growth and life even on badly damaged trees. Species of fungi contain dormant cells that are called into action, "springing to life" following a disaster. Berman assured her that while the forest wouldn't look exactly as it had before, it would certainly return. "Even five years from now, it's going to be green again," he said. "It's going to be lush again."[39]

People are not trees, but the relentless recovery of nature is encouraging in the aftermath of trauma. Recovery is not an immediate return to pre-trauma ways of being with no change, but rather the ability to resume living and functioning in the world in ways that share resemblance to living and functioning pre-trauma.[40] An example is that of a church rebuilding after a fire destroyed its building, painstakingly restoring stained glass and re-creating structures and interior details that had been lost without making significant structural change.

Recovery is a normal response to trauma, and this aspect of resilience can take time. Even when a redwood forest, an individual, or a community takes years to mend and return to some semblance of the old life, we can celebrate the God-given gift of resilience.

Resistance

Wanting to continue living and functioning during and after traumatic events can be a normal response. My former student Zeppelin overcame breast cancer a decade before coming to my seminary. Her initial recovery was followed by a passionate call to ministry that became part of her testimony. Her calling evolved and led her from her native Philippines to Ohio, and eventually to Toronto, Ontario. She felt a divine call to pursue a PhD in preaching and become the first woman to teach preaching in her home country. While finishing her MA thesis, she suffered a devastating recurrence. Weak, struggling to walk and inhale enough air for sustained speech, she insisted on continuing with her work.

Concerned, we staged an intervention. Several of us, the director of her program, thesis supervisor, and her friend and former pastor from the Philippines, now a faculty member at the seminary, gathered in my small faculty office. We encouraged her to halt her studies and return home to her family. We spoke bluntly, "If you only have a few months to live, is this how you want to spend it?" Between raspy breaths, she assured us that her answer was yes.

Zeppelin joined a clinical trial, and her cancer went into remission as she completed her thesis and graduated. She decided to pursue her call to the next level. Accepted into a doctoral program at Emmanuel College in Toronto, she moved north eager to begin studies. Within weeks of her arrival, she went to the emergency room with pain and shortness of breath. A scan revealed that her cancer had returned. With the support of faculty, students, and local church members, she continued balancing classes with treatment until she died from complications related to ongoing cancer treatment. Her spirit and faith were strong, but her body simply gave out.

Resistance, or seeming to show no change in the wake of trauma, has at times been viewed as a dysfunctional response. However, recent studies argue for its validity as a sign of resilience.[41] People and communities that respond this way may not need an intervention to help them "face a new reality." In Zeppelin's situation, the support of others allowed her to resist the cancer that was thwarting her deep sense of God's call in her life. Returning to the example of a church destroyed by fire, resistance may be displayed by the congregation continuing to meet at the same time with the same worship structure and keeping up community practices such as fellowship meals following the fire and during months of transition.

Reconfiguration

Reconfiguration may be what most comes to mind when we imagine resilience. When the Seattle Indian Health Board requested additional personal protective equipment during 2020, they were sent a box of body bags. Public health researcher and member of the Pawnee Nation of Oklahoma Abigail Echo-Hawk felt devastated and traumatized by this potent marker devaluing Native American life. Since her employer had no use for the body bags, she transformed one into a traditional ribbon dress to symbolize resilience. The project also became a way for her to process the trauma of the ongoing devaluing of Indigenous life that she sees regularly in her public health work. Indigenous Americans were nearly four times more likely to become infected with COVID-19 and twice as likely to die from it as white Americans.[42]

The dress features intricate symbols and powerful words of affirmation: "I am a tangible manifestation of my ancestors' resiliency."[43] Echo-Hawk has reconfigured an item meant for death into a garment meant for celebrating culture and life, a sign of resilience amidst a devastating season.

Like transforming a body bag into a celebratory dress, the process of reconfiguration involves survivors making significant changes following traumatic stress. Changes may be internal and external and involve adaptations that can help in weathering future traumatic experience.[44] For the congregation that survived the fire, reconfiguration may involve a new building that is significantly different from the old building, or building again in a new location.

LIFE AFTER TRAUMA

The costs of not addressing or processing collective trauma can be grave. Traumatic experiences housed in the body negatively influence present functioning and relationships. We can pass our trauma from person to person and from generation to generation. Trauma impacts both our nature in a genetic way and our nurture in how we relate to others. Unattended traumatic responses can be cumulative, so that traumatic responses may become more severe in subsequent generations.[45] Our responses today may represent inflamed wounds that our ancestors sustained. Our children and grandchildren may similarly bear the brunt of our unaddressed trauma. Unaddressed trauma can manifest in violence in many forms, in a lack of compassion and cruelty. Traumatic crisis can expose the worst that humanity is capable of as collective trauma dehumanizes and disempowers us through scattering and isolation.

And yet God has seen and continues to see us through experiences of trauma. Mechanisms for processing individual and collective trauma are often instinctual and part of how our bodies have been created. As I explore below, living in the aftermath of trauma involves efforts such as reconstructing systems and trust, remembering, building relationships, and making plans with a sense of both realism and responsibility. Working through collective trauma is something that unfolds naturally for many groups. Addressing trauma need not feel like another responsibility for already-burdened leaders. God is breathing life toward our individual and collective wounds. Even for communities who have layers of generational traumatic stress, in God's timeline it is never too late to experience goodness and life. This gift is extended to all creation.

Reconstruction

When the immediate danger of the traumatic event recedes, survivors often seek to gather the fragments and construct or reconstruct meaningful culture. Healthy cultural patterns and practices can rebuild trust and human connection and help shelter people from the long-term wounding impact of collective trauma, nurturing resilience over time.[46]

Rituals, particularly around grief and bereavement, and stories of survival in the face of crises can sustain and empower us as we heal and mend ties and connections that have broken or frayed. These events often have a deep collective impact. Cultural examples include rituals around showings of the traveling AIDS memorial quilt, spontaneous memorials like the flowers around the gates of Kensington Palace after Princess

Diana died, or the murals, flowers and mementos left at the site where George Floyd was killed.[47]

These practices are familiar to people of faith. We have powerful identity-forming rituals that gather us together, not merely as a local manifestation of the body of Christ, but also with Christian brothers and sisters around the world and the communion of saints. Not only are churches positioned to weather and heal collective trauma faced by congregations, but congregations can also be leaders in broader more systemic situations of collective trauma.

Remembering

An experience of mass trauma often incites the broad social imperative to "never forget." Remembering, reflecting, and reconstructing cultural trauma that has harmed groups allows people to locate causes for the trauma and deeply validate suffering. The study of cultural trauma highlights "meaningful and causal relationships between previously unrelated events, structures, perceptions, and actions." These new relationships can open up pathways of "social responsibility and political action." Exploration of cultural trauma also invites members of a group who may have caused the trauma to take responsibility for it morally and actively, and even experience solidarity with the traumatized culture.[48]

For example, since 2013, Orange Shirt Day has brought attention to the residential school system in Canada and its impact on Indigenous people for more than a century. Residential schools were a systematic part of the colonial settlement of North America. Indigenous children were separated from their families to dismantle and destroy culture and integrate subsequent generations into the colonial project. In the spring of 2021, the remains of more than two hundred children were discovered in an unmarked grave near the Kamloops Residential School in British Columbia, which cast global attention on acts of genocide enacted against Indigenous people in North America. Media scrutiny highlighted past acts by government and religious institutions as well as ongoing effects that continue to manifest in Indigenous communities. September 20, 2021, marked the first statutory observance of Orange Shirt Day, also known as the National Day for Truth and Reconciliation in Canada.[49] All Canadians were encouraged to wear orange and participate in educational and somber commemorative events across Canada.[50]

Relationships

Banding together as one can be a powerful tool for addressing cultural trauma. In a sense, it says "Your suffering is my suffering. You are not alone." As professor of sociology Jeffrey Alexander puts it, solidarity related to suffering and cultural trauma "expands the circle of the we."[51] Solidarity deepens our need to respond.

Jewish philosopher Avishai Margalit writes about agency and trust in "thick" human relationships that move us away from trite sentimentality, which is sometimes associated with language around solidarity, toward something deeper. In the midst of difficult experiences groups can exist in a mode of either fate or destiny. Drawing from the work of Rabbi Joseph Soloveitchik, Margalit asserts that fate is when a person or group is passively acted upon by outside forces, whereas destiny involves agency and the person or group actively seeking to shape life in the midst of these external, usually negative forces. Fate can feel hopeless, fatalistic, while destiny connotes calling, vocation, and choice. These distinctions lead Soloveitchik to two "sacramental covenants," one of fate, which draws from shared suffering, and the other of destiny, which draws from a shared sense of vocation or calling. Margalit uses these descriptions of fate and destiny to deepen our understanding of the concept of solidarity. He writes,

> Solidarity of fate tends to stress victimhood and belongs very much to the culture of victimization; solidarity of destiny tends to be based on responsibility as a historical agent and on pride.
>
> Solidarity of fate consists of allegiance to those who share the common fate. Solidarity of destiny consists of allegiance to a common cause. In the case of solidarity of destiny, it seems as if human relations are bedimmed and the allegiance seems to be an allegiance to a cause. But the cause only helps in forming solidarity: solidarity is predominantly a relation between human beings.
>
> Fate and destiny form two different orientations in time: fate is oriented toward the past, destiny toward the future. Solidarity of fate creates a community of memory, whereas solidarity of destiny creates movement and collective action. When fate and destiny are united and solidarity is a combined force of memory and action, solidarity is in full force.
>
> Solidarity, be it solidarity of fate or of destiny, covers a whole gamut of human emotions. It may begin with mild sympathy, then move to thoroughly intense sympathy involved with moral support, and end with total alignment with a group, which includes readiness for personal sacrifice for the sake of solidifying the relationships in the group.
>
> But solidarity is more than a heap of emotions; it is an entire life stance toward people and ideals.[52]

Realism and responsibility

Solidarity is hard work and not for the faint of heart. Leaders need to be realistic about the time it can take for a congregation to align itself fully with a group beyond the walls of the church. Solidarity involves feelings, relationship, mutuality, investment of time and resources, and direct action over the long haul.

An incident of hate directed against the mosque in Harrisonburg, Virginia, provided an opportunity for Christians and Jews to express solidarity with their faith neighbors. Prior to the COVID-19 pandemic, more than thirty faith communities collaborated as part of the Open Doors program to provide temporary shelter, a meal, and take-out snacks during cold winter months.[53] The program started in 2007, growing from an interfaith association and clergy task force. Houses of worship took turns serving as host for a week at a time, with other communities assisting with volunteers and food. Common acts of kindness and understanding passed among the different faith traditions—for example, the mosque or synagogue would host during Christmas to accommodate Christian groups. Collaboration nurtured relationships and built solidarity over time. When the Islamic Center of the Shenandoah Valley was vandalized in the fall of 2012, their Christian and Jewish friends from Open Doors helped clean and repair.

Of course, unrealistic expectations around time and commitment are not the only challenges of ministering toward solidarity. Far too often, groups with a hand in causing cultural trauma refuse to study or recognize their own role in causing the suffering of others. This deepens the suffering of the traumatized group, invalidates their experiences, and devalues their humanity.

When a group that is responsible for cultural trauma refuses to acknowledge or accept responsibility, it illustrates a horrific expansion of the phenomenon of "gaslighting." Those who do this too often not only refuse to accept responsibility for collective actions that have harmed others, but even blame the traumatized for their own suffering.[54] Not taking responsibility harms those who caused harm as well, with the erosion of physical health, relationships, and morality. Pain and damage caused by lack of acknowledgment is corrosive to individuals and society, and the unresolved trauma can be transferred to later generations.

Post-traumatic growth

When a person or group experiences positive transformation after trauma, therapists call it post-traumatic growth, or PTG. This concept is deeply challenging because traumatic stress causes comprehensive suffering, and for some the suffering is intense and ongoing. For those who survive and resume some semblance of their previous existence, the oft-quoted adage "What doesn't kill you makes you stronger" can feel trite and callous.

When a concept is difficult, art and poetry can help where language fails. Post-traumatic growth can be likened to the Japanese art form kintsugi, a way of repairing broken pottery with molten precious metals that harden to restore shape and function to the piece. The hardened metal leaves beautiful gleaming trails marking where the piece was formerly broken. A worthless broken bowl is transformed into precious art. Observing kintsugi reminds me of the chorus from Leonard Cohen's song "Anthem." Cohen urges his listeners to accept the limitations and "cracks" that inevitably come with being human. The "cracks" open us up so that the "light" can shine in.[55]

Examples of positive transformation following trauma stretch back as far as we have experiences recorded, and we see it in scripture. For example, in the Old Testament, Joseph and Moses grow in calling, relationship with God, and leadership following traumatic experiences. In the New Testament, the experience of early Christians following the traumatic death of Jesus also illustrates not only resilience but post-traumatic growth.

In mentioning post-traumatic growth here, I'm not seeking to invalidate the many negative and often comprehensive effects of trauma or to set people up with expectations for themselves or their loved ones. As one researcher puts it, "Negative events tend to produce, for most persons, consequences that are negative."[56] Life is not a scale where growth or new understanding can ever outweigh loss.

However, studies demonstrate that many individuals and groups do experience growth in the aftermath of trauma. Researchers liken traumatic stress to an earthquake that damages or destroys a building. As long as one must rebuild the building and one has support and resources, why not build it stronger? I have witnessed post-traumatic growth in my own family and in interactions with friends who have survived trauma. Survivors can experience positive changes in their self-perception, relationships, and outlook.[57] Examples include a career change oriented towards helping others or seeking to address suffering in our world.

Yet, despite the measurable growth and meaningful change that many describe, almost all of those surveyed by researchers would give up these positive changes and growth if only the traumatic event or crisis could be undone. This reminds us not to "bright-side" any experience of pain, trauma, or loss.[58] Not even our own, because it denies the complexity of living. We cannot undo the past; we must live in the tension of traumatic wounding and the potential and possibility of growth and change that we can name the light of love, the light of God shining into the cracks.

As with the transformed kintsugi pottery, the experiences
we have in life change and shape us. This is a lifelong process.
Experiences of suffering influence our understanding of who
God is toward us. Essential aspects of God's nature of love,
mercy, and promise-keeping surely remain constant, but God's
interaction with creation can change. The incarnation of God
in Christ brings experiences of suffering and death into the
experience of God in ways that deeply affect God. On this side
of the realm of God, there is a creative tension between loss
and living. It is a tension inherent in the cross and resurrection,
events that exist eternally in the life of God in Jesus Christ.

Resurrection

The event of Jesus' resurrection shows God's deep investment
in life beyond trauma. While we wish we could undo tragic
experiences that create the soil for post-traumatic growth, we
can celebrate positive transformation after trauma as a sign of
God's resurrection power here and now.

Theologian Shelly Rambo's work captures the complexity of holding together life and death, joy and pain. Rambo
expresses this tension in her trauma-informed theology of
resurrection, *Resurrecting Wounds*. Rambo works toward a
theology of resurrection that makes a difference for those suffering here and now, and she insists on a theology that honors
wounds that remain in the wake of traumatic experience.

Rambo writes about the wounds that remain on the resurrected body of Christ. These wounds are to be acknowledged
as part of the risen Jesus, touched as modeled by disciple
Thomas, and not erased because of our theological or aes-
thetic discomfort. These wounds become the soil from which
healing and transformation may emerge with the presence
of the Spirit. Resurrection life is marked by wounds but also

transformed, "recreated."[59] Hidden wounds that surface need
to be attended, not plastered over. Attention to these surfacing
wounds is key in a season of collective trauma where the crisis
of the pandemic has brought many other wounds to the surface,
wounds of inequity, poverty, and racism. Both the wounds and
the path to healing are collective.

Moving forward in the wake of trauma does not mean
that what happened is erased. It means that we live, carrying
our losses and experiences with us, not in a way that fully
defines but as part of our ongoing growth and formation.
Rambo sees the gift of the Spirit breathed upon the disciples in the upper room as creating a new community in the
aftermath of trauma. "The disciples come to terms with the
past and reorient themselves to practices of care and truth
telling. New configurations of life are envisioned and carried
forward."[60]

*   *   *

The experience of a global pandemic is a reminder of how
connected people are. International borders and personal
boundaries were no match for the virus. So too, traumatic
events can radiate far beyond an initial sphere of impact.

Unattended trauma, whether individual or collective, does
not disappear. Pain and brokenness leach out, like toxic chem-
icals poisoning all they touch. Traumatic stress is comprehensive, affecting body, soul, and mind. Collective trauma
unravels our self-understanding, relationships, worldview, and
sense of future possibilities. We may become brittle and frozen; our ability to extend empathy and compassion may suffer.
Studies show that trauma affects our genes so that unmetabo-
lized traumatic stress can be passed down to future generations.

Traumatic responses are complex and multifaceted. Traumatic stress can impact societal patterns, economics, and politics. Broken trust associated with trauma may cause some to opt out of political participation altogether and lead others to gravitate toward authoritarian political structures with a strong leader who consolidates power.

Moving forward in a way that processes collective trauma necessitates self-awareness and reflection. For some congregations, moving forward may take the shape of completely new ministries, such as continuing to have worship and other church events online as well as face to face, or a desire to utilize church facilities in a new way to explore what the physicality of a building represents for a community including and beyond the congregation itself. Moving forward may involve a deeper sense of connection to God and freedom within the community as well as solidarity with others leading to a shared sense of God's calling.

Churches can provide a source of strength and resilience amidst the corrosive effects of chronic trauma. Just as food can sometimes buffer a body against harmful side effects of a medication, numerous studies show that participation in worship has a buffering effect that nurtures resilience even as chronic trauma continues.[61]

The subsequent chapters explore three practices that may contribute to this buffering effect. Lament, storytelling, and blessing can help facilitate and encourage holistic metabolization of mass trauma. These chapters may be used as personal practices, tools for families, a guide for small groups, or the structure for a worship or Christian education series. While trauma healing is not often a linear process, these practices represent general areas that research has shown to be conducive to processing trauma and embracing life in meaningful ways.

TWO

Lament

A mentor of mine often reminded students that we are dust infused with the very breath of God—inviting us into the richness of holding those realities together. This identity, dust infused with divine breath, lies at the heart of the biblical practice of lament. Lament is a deep prayer practice that can engage a wide range of experiences. Within the biblical tradition of lament, we find aspects of grief and protest, anger and praise, deep trust in God alongside questioning God, and testimony to the sovereignty of God amidst the perils and promise of being human.

In September 2021, the art installation *In America: Remember*, consisting of more than 670,000 small white flags, was installed on over twenty acres of federal park land on the National Mall.[1] Visitors described the sight from a distance as reminiscent of water or sequins as the hundreds of thousands of flags glinted and waved in the wind and sun. The sheer number of flags made a powerful impression taken together, but each flag was inscribed by hand with the name of a person who died from COVID-19, and some of the names were accompanied by stories.[2] Artist Suzanne Brennan Firstenberg emphasized the importance of something physical to mark the scope of our collective loss. She encouraged visitors to imagine the concentric circles of loss that surround each flag: family members, friends, work colleagues, members of a house of worship.[3]

Having a physical place to go and something physical to mark loss can help contain what feels intangible and can give people permission to express deep emotions connected to a profound loss of life.

The exhibit at the National Mall was important, but many people lack access to such spaces, and as the number of lives lost to COVID has continued, there has not been a significant collective response. A bill that would have declared a National Day of Mourning has stalled in the US Congress.[4] In a culture that tends to focus on relentless positivity, lament seems to be a forgotten practice.

Nevertheless, the drive to concretize and attend to grief and loss is persistently human. An artist in Brentwood, Maryland, created an interactive exhibit riffing on the lost-and-found boxes that are a staple of many schools, churches, and break rooms to help her neighbors process their experiences associated with the cascade of trauma and loss in 2020.[5] The exhibit served as a memorial of sorts. It consisted of boxes decorated by selected neighbors and small tags offered to anyone who wished to participate, all affixed to a fence. The tags and mementos expressed losses such as the death of loved ones, loss of in-person school and social relationships, missed experiences, connections, and beloved habits. The exhibit also witnessed to that which was discovered or recovered, such as adopting a new pet, new closeness with siblings, or a hobby such as sewing or crocheting learned or relearned. For several months, the living and evolving art piece served as a memorial, a protest, and even a celebration. The items and tags on the fence became a means to begin to process complex experiences of powerlessness, loss, choices, and hope, a reminder of the complexities of what it is to be human and all the associated promise and frailty.

The practice of lament allows believers to be vulnerable, to name brokenness, need, and inability to move forward. There are very few spaces where this kind of radical honesty is possible. North American culture encourages denial of negative feelings or responses. A massive self-help industry tells us to paint on a smile and model a can-do attitude, even amid extreme loss. We long for a quick fix—an easy path to well-being—and are extremely uncomfortable admitting that we are anything other than happy, capable, and the picture of complete mental and physical health. The self-help industry takes advantage of struggling people by offering consumption as an easy answer. In a recent interview, trauma social worker and educator Laura van Dernoot Lipsky noted the challenge that Americans face with grief and mourning: "We don't talk about loss. By and large, it's all about consumption to help numb you out."[6]

In addition to the associated collateral health and financial problems that can arise from using consumption as a crutch for pain, denying essential aspects of humanity can also serve as a shield that keeps us from acknowledging our vulnerability and experiencing the love and closeness that comes from authentic relationships between imperfect people.[7]

The Bible itself is full of sin, pain, brokenness, trauma, and lament. The old hymn "What a Friend We Have in Jesus" has that wonderful phrase: "all our sins and griefs to bear." However, the church has not always been a space where deep pain can be voiced. Even talking about the deep pain that lies at the heart of the gospel itself—Jesus' horrific death on a Roman cross—is controversial for some believers. A recent conversation with a friend who serves in leadership for children's ministry at her church expressed frustration around a parent complaining that Jesus' death had been mentioned during a children's activity. The parent felt that the world was just "too sad right now" to also talk about Jesus' death. Somehow this parent had sadly missed the deep comfort of connection with our triune God who has experienced suffering and death, has experienced the agonizing death of a loved one, and who continues to groan and cry out with the suffering of God's beloved world.

RECOVERING LAMENT

Lament is a primal expression of human anguish and protest. From a perspective of faith, lament is an act of prayer. It is inherently social, involving not only the one or ones praying but also God and a surrounding community of listeners and individuals who bear witness to the lament and may be moved to personal prayer and action.[8] Biblical lament is an act of protest, expressing grief, anxiety, rage, and complaint to God.[9]

Following traumatic events, it has become the custom for politicians and other leaders to express that "thoughts and prayers" are with those directly affected. One of the results of this habit is that many have come to see language around prayer as empty and ineffective—a substitute for direct action. But believers hold that prayer is not empty or ineffective.

Still, lament has slipped into disuse in corporate worship and private prayer. Even when pastors include psalms of lament in worship, some may miss depth and potential within the practice. Many believers are not familiar with lament. However, when people feel powerless amid pain and suffering, prayers of lament can emerge as an action that can be taken when people feel incapable of anything else. A recovery of lament may help to rehabilitate prayer as a fitting response after trauma.

Recovering the practice of lament has the potential to restore a vital tool for deepening connection to God and others. It may help congregations process complex experiences connected to mass trauma. And lament may help empower bystander witnesses to act for justice on behalf of those who are suffering.

Prayers of lament can be offered together in worship or small group settings or by individuals at home or in a situation of grief or loss such as a hospital waiting room, the ICU, or a funeral home. Hurting people can be completely honest with God. Our loving God has chosen to be in relationship with humanity and has promised to save and restore us.

This chapter offers a brief introduction to the prayerful practice of lament. I will unpack some reasons why lament is underutilized in many ministry settings and examine important theological claims associated with lament. Biblical patterns of lament will serve as a guide, tool, and anchor for how the present practice of lament might function in congregations. The chapter will also offer suggestions and examples of how congregations, small groups, and individuals can practice lament today as a means of processing collective trauma and other experiences of pain, brokenness, and loss.

BIBLICAL PRACTICES OF LAMENT

Biblical laments incorporate the primal response of people suffering, within the context of scripture that testifies to God's power and ongoing engagement with people. Scriptural laments can feel more like public protests than the staid corporate prayers that may typically happen in Sunday morning worship. Biblical laments point out ruptures in the fabric of the world—places where systems and structures are doing harm or not addressing need. When situations of injustice reach an intolerable level, ordinary and brave people lay their bodies on the line to expose and protest injustices perpetrated against other bodies.[10] Biblical laments also bring vulnerable human bodies into the presence of power, in this case our God, who responds to the cries of people and acts in our world.

After the police attacked peaceful protesters on the Edmund Pettus Bridge on "Bloody Sunday," March 7, 1965, thousands flocked to Selma to link arms, sing, and advocate for voting rights as they marched to Montgomery. These acts of sacrifice, worship, protest, and advocacy can be understood as modern practices of lament.

There are two primary expressions of lament in the Bible, prayerful plea and dirge.[11] (These categories are not mutually exclusive.) Psalms of lament tend to follow a kind of basic pattern of a prayerful plea with three major movements.[12] Nearly half the psalms contain lament. Psalm 6 is one example. The psalmist is crying out to God for help in a time when life is under threat and the psalmist is suffering intensely.

- *Addressing God.* This emphasizes the covenant relationship and the person or people's right to ask for God's action. Psalm 6:1: "O LORD."
- *Lament, petition, God's motivations.* This involves naming the painful situation, directly appealing to God to act, and potentially naming reasons for God to intervene, such as God's past intervention or maintaining God's reputation. Psalm 6:2, 4–5: "Be gracious to me, O LORD, for am I languishing; O LORD, heal me, for my bones are shaking with terror. . . . Turn, O LORD, save my life; deliver me for the sake of your steadfast love.

For in death there is no remembrance of you; in Sheol who can give you praise?"

- *Praise that God has heard and thankfulness for God's action.* Psalm 6:8–10, "Depart from me, all you workers of evil, for the LORD has heard the sound of my weeping. The LORD has heard my supplication; the LORD accepts my prayer. All my enemies shall be ashamed and struck with terror; they shall turn back, and in a moment be put to shame."

The entire act of lament is relational, beginning with a focus on relationship and a sense of understanding that God cares about creaturely suffering and moving to a deep sense of trust that God will respond.[13] This grounds lament theologically in the context of ongoing connection between God and people.

Many scholars have explored how psalmists made this prayerful transition from anguished cry to deep trust and praise. Some hold that lament psalms were experienced in liturgical contexts in which God speaks perhaps through a priest or prophetic oracle. Others see the very announcement of God's hearing and acting made at the end as a kind of guarantee that help is on the way. Still another theory is that speaking the name of God itself is enough to evoke a deep change.[14]

The dirge form of lament is less common in the Bible. It is used to mark deep grief on the occasion of death or loss; for example, David laments the deaths of Saul and Jonathan in 2 Samuel 1:17–27.[15] This form of lament was also appropriated by biblical prophets. For example, Jeremiah's grief for Israel extends to the whole of creation. "I looked on the earth, and lo, it was waste and void; and to the heavens, and they had no light. I looked on the mountains, and lo, they were quaking, and all the hills moved to and fro. I looked, and lo, there was no one at all, and all the birds of the air had fled. I looked, and lo, the fruitful land was a desert, and all its cities were laid in ruins before the LORD, before his fierce anger. . . . Because of this the earth shall mourn" (Jeremiah 4:23–26, 28a).

At one time the psalms were regularly used as personal devotional prayers for individuals. Praying lament psalms can provide the words we ourselves may lack in a moment of crisis. (This practice is detailed later in the chapter.) A pastor friend regularly reminds me that when we pray the psalms we do not pray alone. We pray with generations of faithful believers. Experiences of trauma can lead to isolation. In times of intense anguish, we may pray with the psalmist and the cloud of witnesses across time,

> O Lord, all my longing is known to you;
>   my sighing is not hidden from you.
> My heart throbs, my strength fails me;
>   as for the light of my eyes—it also has gone from me.
> My friends and companions stand aloof from my affliction,
>   and my neighbors stand far off.
> (Psalm 38:9–11)

IMPLICIT LAMENT IN OUR WORLD

Lament is an instinctual act that helps us stay fully human during deeply painful situations and experiences. While lament has grown less common in corporate worship and private devotions for a wide variety of reasons, as we'll explore in part below, expressing lament is a human need that finds expression in our world, particularly among people who have experienced systemic injustice and oppression.

Professor of Christian education Anne Streaty Wimberly helpfully voices implicit actions of lament with a focus on Black experience. Silence, anguished cries, expressions of fear, and of rage, unfold in our world with heartbreaking regularity. Naming these responses intentionally as lament allows the church to embrace these responses theologically as prayer and protest before a God who cares and responds with liberating power. Intentionally engaging these expressions is also deeply validating and empowering for those who are suffering.

Silence

Traumatic experiences often push us beyond the realm of language. Silence can be an expression of lament in several modes. In the immediate aftermath of shock or traumatic experiences, it can feel as though the breath has been siphoned from one's body. Words are not possible. Hearing the news of a sudden tragedy can often elicit this form of silent lament.[16] Those who remember the assassinations of John Kennedy and Martin Luther King Jr. may recall being without words. When the World Trade Center towers fell in New York City on September 11, seasoned broadcasters struggled to describe to their audiences what was unfolding. Naming this silence as lament gives a sense of agency and meaning to this innate response.

Another form of silent lament involves active physical motion.[17] We may not have words, but our bodies may express prayers of lament. One thinks of family members pacing the halls in a hospital, wringing their hands, and waiting to hear from doctors. Rocking or swaying alone or with others can express lament. Immediately following the murder of Martin Luther King Jr., Walter Cronkite described crowds silently spilling into the streets of Harlem.[18] Gathering together, standing in vigil, marching in a street can all be claimed as silent forms of lament.

Sadly, too many survivors have not had a choice in their silence. Coerced silencing is often enacted upon people by

systems under threat. Sometimes this can take the form of a
nondisclosure agreement signed as part of a legal settlement.
Sometimes this happens when someone keeps quiet due to fear
of retribution, such as a young Black man who says nothing
while being racially profiled and stopped by the police.[19] In
some circumstances of domestic violence a survivor says nothing to avoid provoking more abuse.

After the fact, those who have been silenced amid the trauma
of systemic injustice or other forms of violence can reclaim
agency by naming it as a type of lament. Congregations can
express solidarity in corporate prayer with those who have
been silenced, "God, we lament the silenced cries of our brothers and sisters in situations of abuse. Protect them, place your
arms around them, provide a way to safety and freedom."

Anguished cries

Wordless cries and groans can be expressions of grief, pain,
lament, and protest. Scripture promises us that the Holy Spirit
intercedes for us in these groans that exist beyond language
(Romans 8:26). Womanist theologian A. Elaine Crawford
claims the "holler" in particular as a form of lament in the
Black community. "The Holler is the primal cry of pain, abuse,
violence, separation. It is a soul-piercing shrill . . . the renunci-
ation of racialized and genderized violence perpetrated against
them generation after generation. The Holler is a cry to God to
'come see about me' one of your children."[20]

The holler is the soul-wrenching lament of the separation
of mother and child. In Black experience, this includes the
cries of mothers separated from their children who were sold
away during slavery and continues until this day. The holler
is the lament of Hagar, anticipating the death of her son. It is
the cry of Rachel, invoked by Jeremiah and Matthew, "wailing

and loud lamentation. Rachel weeping for her children; she refused to be consoled, because they are no more" (Matthew 2:18; also Jeremiah 31:15). We hear this same cry today in the aftermath of mass shootings. We hear it in the cries of Samaria Rice, Gwen Carr, Tamika Palmer, and Wanda Cooper-Jones, mothers mourning Black children murdered by the police. George Floyd's own anguished cry for his mother moments before his life was crushed from him is an expression of the holler. Anne Streaty Wimberly describes her own holler of lament at the death of her first child in the 1960s, "having been left unattended in my own vomit on a stretcher in the hospital hallway because there was no room in the 'colored wing' and being sent to the 'White wing'" was prohibited."[21]

The holler specifically speaks to Black experience, but the maternal cry of anguished and wrenching loss exists as a primal and broadly human expression of lament. My husband's cousin described this cry when their infant daughter, Nora died after protracted illness.[22] The response was spontaneous and instinctual even though her death was not unexpected.

Expressions of fear

Certain expressions of fear, particularly in communities facing oppression, can also be understood as lament. Howard Thurman writes eloquently about fear as "one of the persistent hounds of hell that dog the footsteps of the poor, the dispossessed, the disinherited."[23] For survivors of trauma, fear can be an expression of humanity in inhumane settings. To feel fear is to remember that there can also be a time without fear. During Russia's assault on Ukraine in early 2022, the circumstances for civilians changed instantly from regular life to a constant state of vigilance and fear punctuated by suffering and death. In Kharkiv, a photographer captured the image of a loaf of bread on a park bench dusted with snow, a puddle of blood nearby bearing witness. Two lives were ended abruptly during a mortar attack. The man and woman were sharing a late lunch and a neighbor in a nearby apartment was putting on her kettle for tea when her windows shuddered with the force of the explosion.[24] Most of the residents were afraid to speak with the reporters, afraid of Russian retaliation. To fear is to lament present danger, to know that this is not how God intended people to live. We pray, "Kyrie eleison!" We pray, "Dear God, do not let fear be the last word! May your mercy, your peace, and your perfect love fill this place!"

Placing intense feelings of fear and injustice in the context of a loving God's vision for human flourishing that seems absent inspires lament. When Asian Americans express fear in walking the streets alone after racialized attacks, when my Black colleague expresses fear at the sight of a police vehicle, and when my students fear for the lives of their teenage Black sons, lament honors these experiences and calls upon God to intervene.

First John reminds us that perfect love that comes from God towards us casts out fear: when experiences of fear threaten to overtake us or others, we can pray for God's love (1 John 4:18).

Viewing expressions of fear as potential prayers of lament can be a means of releasing our fear into God's hands. God's good news announcing Jesus' birth came to the poor and dis-inherited with words of comfort, "Fear not!" (Luke 2:10 KJV).

However, God's fear-shattering love is not a Band-Aid or a pacifier that gets us by for a moment. God's love is transformative, leading us to change racist systems and practices that generate fear.

Rage

We've seen the images flashing across our screens. Neighbor-hoods burning, stores being looted, property destroyed. For those who have not directly experienced deep injustice and racialized trauma directly, these responses can be hard to watch and understand.

Rage is a trauma response. Destructive rage can erupt when groups have been treated inhumanely and have no agency through official or socially acceptable channels of action. Destructive rage can harm the self and others. Following George Floyd's murder, many were rightly filled with rage.

Constructive rage can be a form of lament and a means to process trauma, an audacious act that testifies amidst the rubble of unjust circumstances. Within the frame of Black experience, Wimberly describes this as "Black people's anger of 'explosive lashing out' when Black people's backs are against the wall." Constructive rage offers "radical critique of injustice, calls out the necessity of change, and evokes the will to change reality."[25]

In the tradition of biblical lament as a means of protest and questioning God, constructive rage sounds in the voices of people questioning unjust systems in ways that spark change. The psalmist cries to God, "Pour out your anger on the nations that do not know you, and on the kingdoms that do not call on your name. For they have devoured Jacob and laid waste his habitation" (Psalm 79:6–7). Sojourner Truth asks, "Ain't I a woman?" Martin Luther King Jr. bears witness: "America has given the Negro people a bad check, a check which has come back marked insufficient funds." Fannie Lou Hamer declares, "I am sick and tired of being sick and tired."[26]

LAMENT AS COMPLEX SOCIAL ACT

Because the voice and perspective of lament psalms are so vulnerable and raw, it can be easy to forget that the psalter served as Israel's collective worship book. In North American culture, many of us tend to keep our most tender or uncomfortable emotions private. When I imagine the emergence of a lament prayer such as Psalm 13, I picture an individual agonizing in darkness, on their knees or prostrate on the ground, pouring out their pain to God. However, lament is also a complex social and relational act. Lament is prayer emerging from pain in the context of relationship, directed towards God, that can be offered by individuals or groups. W. Derek Suderman pushes us a step further by highlighting that there is also a "third party," beyond God and the one or ones actively lamenting. There is a social audience for lament, the ones who listen and in whose presence this prayer may occur.[27]

Suderman builds on the work of Walter Brueggemann, who encourages the reclamation of lament to give voice to those who are often silenced and to challenge patterns and systems that contribute to oppression and suffering.[28] Lament offers a powerful countermelody to a prevailing cultural tune that supports the status quo: Everything is fine. Don't change a thing.

The social function of lament can draw attention to places where God may be calling communities to respond and connect both within and beyond. Laments can be directed to God against other people, to God against God, and to other people. Psalm 55 speaks about the betrayal of a "friend," clearly calling out to God but also challenging the friend and engaging in this prayerful complaint in a social setting where others would have surely borne witness as well. We can trace the party the psalmist addresses by tracking through the psalm to note places where pronouns shift.[29] In 55:13, the psalmist addresses his betrayer directly. In verse 16, the psalmist speaks of God in the third person, suggesting a broader social circle as the recipients of his lament. In the final verse, the address returns to directly speaking to God.

For lament to do its important work, a community is necessary. Suderman highlights the relational connection for those who are active witnesses to lament. For those surrounding the complainant, laments can function as "warnings, threats, accusations, and appeals for empathy and support."[30]

The church as a discerning community is not merely a passive observer of these cries. The church is a community where lament still has a powerful function to move people to action. Suderman argues that "it is not only the case that lament challenges God to take the 'petitionary party' seriously, but the voice of lament requires its social audience to do the same. . . . Must the faith community sit on its hands and wait for heaven to act?"[31] Scripture, history, tradition, and experience tell us the answer is *no*. Lament affects not only heavenly but also earthly listeners; God can and does act through humans to change situations here and now.

In the presence of lament, one cannot remain neutral. The anguish of those wronged and suffering begs response. To witness vulnerability and pain transforms us and cracks us open. We recognize our own tender and broken places.

Professor emeritus of preaching Tom Long recounts a story of wordless collective lament and witness in his sermon "Troubled," preached at a continuing education event for preachers held by Calvin Seminary. The village of Dachau, Germany, was the site of a concentration camp with over thirty thousand documented deaths of people. Today the site is a memorial and a museum. Long describes a picture that hangs in a gallery visitors file past. The picture is of a woman and her daughter walking to the gas chambers. The woman is using the only agency that she has to protest this cruelty and protect her child. She is covering her child's eyes with her hands. Long believes that all who pass this photograph are moved to pray, and the prayer is a cry of lament, "O God, don't let this be the last word!"[32]

Kaethe Weingarten's work with compassionate witness offers additional pathways to response. While "toxic witness" ignores the resonant cries that rise up within us with another being's sufferings, "compassionate witness" intentionally reflects and engages with the pain of another, then thoughtfully and purposely seeks action either symbolic or actual in response that takes into account the full humanity of the hurting and those who witness.[33]

For example, in response to the lament of loved ones who were unable to visit relatives in a nursing home for many months and who may have not been able to be present at the time of death due to the COVID-19 pandemic, a symbolic action may involve creating a visual memorial to those loved ones—either online or in a space at church or outside church—with pictures and mementos. This visual act can be acknowledged and brought into the whole fellowship with a responsive prayer created for worship.

Congregants may also extend acts of care towards those who lost loved ones by offering meals or the gift of a prayer shawl or handmade blanket to symbolize the love of the community. Less symbolic action may involve donating money or personal protective equipment resources to a nursing care facility, or providing gift cards, baked goods, or flowers as a thank you to those who worked on nursing care facilities and provided loving touch.

LAMENT, TRAUMA, AND LIBERATION

For survivors of trauma, lament is especially important because it maintains relationship between survivors and God, thus combating a sense of isolation and alienation. Even when it seems there is no answer from God, responding to painful experiences through lament fosters a sense of connection and resilience. Lament also clearly names the pain, which may begin to help survivors process or make sense of the situation at their own speed and pacing. Finally, lament provides a sense of voice and active agency that has been stolen by the traumatic event or events.

In a situation of collective trauma, lament may be the only appropriate response we can make initially. In a *Time* magazine article written in the late spring 2020, biblical scholar N. T. Wright reminds readers that lament asks questions but receives no definitive answers. It does not minimize pain and loss. It does not explain them away. The human act of lament is an echo of God's own lament, attested by scripture in both the Old and New Testaments. Wright makes an important link between lament and our very vocation as Christians: "It is no part of the Christian vocation, then, to be able to explain what's happening and why. In fact, it is part of the Christian vocation not to be able to explain—and to lament instead. As the Spirit laments within us, so we become, even in our self-isolation, small shrines where the presence and healing love of God can dwell."[34]

Biblical lament offers a path to bring scripture and theology into conversation with experiences of suffering and trauma in an embodied and honest way. Preachers don't need to downplay the agony of the text or find a way to ascribe easy theological answers that are ultimately unhelpful. Biblical laments keep us from becoming numb to the risks and realities of being human.

Traumatic experience can bind survivors with a power the trauma doesn't deserve. Lament can help facilitate an experience of liberation. Breaking free from harmful behaviors and patterns related to trauma is a crucial part of experiencing life more fully.

Anne Streaty Wimberly names the shouts of African American protesters, "I can't breathe!" and "Black lives matter!", as cries of lament. She encourages congregations to give permission for people to cry, to "form and express the language of lament." She writes specifically about Black communities, "There must be a coming to grips with woundedness, grief, and lament in ways that release and move us to declare *why* it is important to live, to engage in advocacy, and to demand change." The loving power and presence of God among God's beloved people is the key to being able to proclaim the "why" and move communities from disempowered despair to meaningful action.[35]

RESISTANCE TO LAMENT

If lament is such a potent faith tool, why then is it so rarely embraced as a Christian practice, a topic for Sunday school, or even as a part of regular Sunday worship? The tides of culture, internal resistance to discomfort, and even some aspects of our theology tug us away from this deep biblical practice.

Commitment to self-help and self-sufficiency as resistance to lament

As noted earlier, North American culture has a normative narrative of self-help, "power of positivity," and empowerment. Every day we are bombarded with countless messages that things are getting better, that great things are just around the corner, and that we can fix any difficulty that we face. This narrative is embedded in a marketplace that preys upon us by linking our hope for a better life to the power to purchase or be productive. One of the most insidious harms of this narrative/marketplace mashup is that it robs regular human beings whose lives aren't perpetually "getting better" of beauty, truth, love, and goodness, which are God's gifts to us in the midst of life *as it is*.[36]

Historian Kate Bowler had spent years studying prosperity gospel when her own diagnosis of stage four cancer at the age of thirty-five created a painful dissonance between her reality and cultural messages. Our world often connects worth to productivity and emphasizes our ability to fix ourselves and change our lives for the better. Our culture has a long history of viewing humans as commodities. We live immersed in systems and structures supported by marketing and a desire to sell products. Bowler has since written two memoirs and created a podcast dedicated to what she calls the "chronic condition" of simply being a person.[37]

Bowler begins her weekly podcast, *Everything Happens*, with an astute observation that partly explains reticence toward the act of lament: "The world loves you better when you are shiny, when you are cheerful, when you still believe that your best life now is right around the corner."[38] Part of Bowler's aim in her podcast is to acknowledge that this hoped-for future is, in fact, a mirage for many people and that leaning into that lie causes additional pain in already difficult situations.

Our culture can be cruel and not understanding of truth-tellers who speak honestly about the things that are wrong and painful in our lives and world. Many don't feel safe acknowledging weakness and imperfection. Thus, lament necessitates a level of vulnerability that represents too much of a risk.

People so often feel that they must earn love. To be loved according to this mindset, we must be able to endlessly extend ourselves toward others, be self-sufficient, and be capable. No one wants to be labeled as "needy." As Leonard Cohen puts it, we come to love "like a refugee."[39] In his book *When Tears Sing*, Episcopal priest William Blaine-Wallace emphasizes our discomfort with being part of God's community of "the fragile and resilient." He writes, "We know sufficiency's short half-life—the attainment of an adequate life can be fleeting and is an ever-moving target."[40]

We put a great deal of time and effort into creating and maintaining boundaries that guard our sufficiency and in keeping up at least a veneer that we are indeed happy, healthy, and successful. Living life with an eye towards how it might look on Instagram can play into this desire in deeply insidious ways that further undercut the opportunity to receive support and help when needed.

Avoiding pain as resistance to lament

The truth can hurt. Some of the resistance to lament is a very human tendency to avoid pain. Therapist Resmaa Menakem writes with clarity about the challenge of resistance to processing experiences of collective trauma. Menakem's book *My Grandmother's Hands* addresses the nuances of trauma caused by racism and racialized violence. Processing trauma involves discomfort. Growth and change are hard work; internal and external resistance are natural responses. However, not doing the hard work of processing trauma has potential for greater pain in the long term.

Menakem delineates between these two types of pain by referring to them as "clean pain" and "dirty pain." He writes,

Clean pain is pain that mends and can build your capacity for growth. It's the pain you experience when you know, exactly, what you need to say or do; when you really, really don't want to say or do it; and when you do it anyway. It's also the pain you experience when you have no idea what to do; when you're scared or worried about what might happen; and when you step forward into the unknown anyway, with honesty and vulnerability.

Experiencing clean pain enables us to engage our integrity and tap into our body's inherent resilience and coherence, in a way that dirty pain does not. Paradoxically, only by walking into our pain or discomfort—experiencing it, moving through it, and metabolizing it—can we grow. It's how the human body works.

Clean pain hurts like hell. But it enables our bodies to grow through our difficulties, develop nuanced skills, and mend our trauma. In this process, the body metabolizes clean pain. The body can then settle; more room for growth is created in its nervous system; and the self becomes freer and more capable, because it now has access to energy that was previously protected, bound, and constricted. When this happens, people's lives often improve in other ways as well. . . .

Dirty pain is the pain of avoidance, blame, and denial. When people respond from their most wounded parts, become cruel or violent, or physically or emotionally run away, they experience dirty pain. They also create more of it for themselves and for others.[41]

Lament is an expression of clean pain. Lament represents a moment of radical honesty about painful and deeply unfair experiences, things that have not unfolded according to God's intentions for creation. Too often communities with privilege choose the path of "dirty pain" rather than face entrenchment and investment in systems that perpetuate racism, xenophobia, and misogyny that devalues people.

The concept of collective trauma recognizes that one person's pain impacts others. This is very true in congregations where individuals may have a traumatic experience while others bear witness. For those potentially in the witnessing community, to hear a friend and brother or sister in Christ lament reminds us of the painful realities of our humanity: limits, brokenness, dashed expectations, betrayal, anger, the inevitability of death. These are weighty matters that are tempting to avoid when everything in our lives is going okay. In fact, there can sometimes be fear that the calamity another is experiencing could happen to us if we acknowledge it fully. This is an experience often encountered by survivors of trauma.

Trauma associated with the COVID-19 pandemic is especially insidious in that the virus is actually transmissible, leading to even greater isolation for those who have experienced sickness and death in their families.

Some who have experienced pain and loss desire to move forward and not spend time dwelling with the complex associated feelings. There are many distractions that society rewards—for example, throwing oneself into work, family responsibilities, or even leadership roles. Society shames other distractions, such as substance abuse, overeating, or other compulsive addictive behaviors.

Traditional theology as resistance to lament

For the church in particular, some aspects of theology can silence voices of lament. Here the fault may lie partly with a traditional culture in which theologians were male and were not expected, encouraged, or sometimes even equipped to deal with emotion or acknowledge bodily vulnerability. A lopsided theological focus on the resurrection, God's provision, and God's power can lead to a simplistic and ultimately experientially untrue sense that somehow believers are immune from suffering or bad things because God will protect and save them.

When God's beloved ones are not spared pain and suffering, it is hard to square with these beliefs and can lead to a crisis of faith or a crisis of witness. Like the disciples caught out on the stormy sea with Jesus asleep, we cry out, "Jesus, don't you care!" (Matthew 8:23–27; Mark 4:35–41; Luke 8:22–25).

Some congregations limit lament to very specific settings such as funerals and otherwise focus on praising God and empowering believers to faithful action in the world. These are important, but without lament and an opportunity to acknowledge and name need and brokenness, our praise may feel hollow, and action may feel futile and exhausting. God meets us in our need—this is the experience of grace.[42]

For some believers, it may be easier to stay in a more passive posture of faith, turning to a God who is omnipotent and always to be praised rather than questioned or challenged. Believers can feel ashamed of feelings of doubt or uncertainty. However, doubt and faith are not mutually exclusive. They exist together, as part of our humanity. The ability to doubt may even be understood as a gift from our God, who desires passionate relationship with us as a partner in covenant.[43] God created complicated people like us, not "puppet people" who respond at the pull of a string.

The psalms provide an example. Psalms of lament frequently embrace anger at God and praise of God. Even psalms of thanksgiving, such as Psalm 30, honestly name difficulty and brokenness, a shadow of lament amidst generous praise and thanksgiving. For clergy, preaching on the psalms can highlight these dynamics. For believers, praying the psalms in worship or as part of private devotion can reinforce complex relational dynamics that strengthen resilience and a deeper relationship with God.

The same cultural narratives that encourage a lie about self-sufficiency and productivity place a barrier between us and God. Our Creator loves us in our humanity, limits and all. God embraces humanity fully in the person of Jesus. Jesus didn't focus on self-improvement or "living his best life" or appease those who would see violent resistance to unjust systemic power as a path to a better life. Rather, he embodies complete self-giving love in a way that the world with its self-improvement and productivity-driven narratives of worth and power still struggles to understand.

Late modernity and secularism as resistance to lament

In his critique of some aspects of modern church life, Walter Brueggemann also observes how lament has fallen out of favor. He sees this attrition as rooted in communities that no longer believe that God can and does act in our world or who feel very invested in the present social order.[44] Rather than illustrating a lack of faith in God, lament reveals a deep and strong faith in God's power to act and to change broken lives and broken systems in our world here and now.

For most pastors, part of serving the church in our present late modern/postmodern context involves getting comfortable with diversity of perspective. To use a gardening metaphor, a congregation won't all be tulips or daisies. It is normal and healthy for congregations to hold a range of perspectives that can cross-pollinate with each other. Pastors and leaders can feel pressure to defend God and to prevent bad theology from taking root in the vulnerable soil of people in pain. While this impulse is good, it can cause harm by stifling valid responses to suffering and crisis, limit people's ability to connect with God, and even turn people away from the church. It can also be soul-crushing for pastors! Who wants to spend their precious energies scouring their congregations for theological "weeds"?

While pastors should be careful with theological interpretations in preaching, public prayers, and liturgies, believers are free and possess agency when it comes to expression and relationship with God, particularly in seasons of intense stress. An episode of *The West Wing* artistically renders this kind of frank relationship with God. When President Bartlet's much loved secretary Mrs. Landingham dies in a car accident with a drunk driver, his chief of staff arranges to have the National Cathedral sealed. A faithful Roman Catholic, Bartlet paces the aisle voicing his rage and protest directly to God.[45]

One of the congregations my husband served decided to stop using the creed in worship. This was with the hope of acknowledging real doubts among some worshipers in being able to truthfully affirm all parts of the creed. Not every congregation uses a creedal shorthand to affirm the most crucial aspects of Christianity, but nearly every congregation struggles with the tension between doubt and faith. Worshipers wonder if what the Bible says is really true. Fortunately, doubt and faith are not polar experiences. Lament helps us embody a theological path that can embrace theological diversity in our congregations.

BENEFITS OF LAMENT

Practicing lament can be especially helpful in processing collective trauma. It offers many benefits that can nurture resilience and renewal in congregations. Lament speaks a difficult and unpopular truth about the human experience, but one that can ultimately be liberating and facilitate an experience of God meeting us in love where we are most broken. There are few safe outlets to express lament in our world today—this is a gift that the church can extend.

Physical benefits of lament

Some research has shown that lament can contribute to physical healing for those dealing with symptoms of traumatic stress. While trauma is corrosive to the brain, learning a new skill such as the practice of lament, and creating your own prayers, can help forge new neural pathways in the brain and cause new brain cells to form. Praying lament prayers from the psalms can offer survivors powerful poetic images that move beyond language and can "counteract the toxic trauma memory."[46]

Churches can provide a safe space to learn and express lament. The following are additional benefits for congregations who practice lament.

Social benefits of lament

Corporate lament in public worship builds a sense of solidarity and caring within a community and connects worshipers to those who suffer not only in the present but throughout history. This sense of connection is enhanced through the use of biblical laments. Corporate lament can nurture solidarity and bring issues of injustice and suffering into a broader field of awareness. The practice of corporate lament proclaims loudly, "You are not alone. You are not forgotten."

Faith benefits of lament

When we lament, we follow Jesus' own example of lamenting on the cross. In Jesus, God experiences what it is to be forsaken by God: this means that "God-forsakenness" is no more. No territory or zone of human experience is beyond the presence of God. Jesus' cry of abandonment is simultaneously a proclamation of God entering the most broken places of human existence.[47]

Processing trauma often involves a drive to somehow make sense or find meaning in the aftermath. Dealing with the fall-out of trauma is exhausting. Lament offers grace as it shifts the burden of trying to make sense of what has happened, the weight of pain and unanswered questions, from us to God.[48] Corporate lament makes pain in our world "the public business of God."[49] It calls upon God to act, to "be God" for us. In deep love for us, God accepts and carries this burden for us.

At its core, the practice of lament affirms deep elements of our faith:

1. That God is active in our world. God is doing something—on the move in gracious and good ways.
2. That injustice and brokenness are not a permanent part of creation—the pull of God's redemption is ultimately stronger.

Healing benefits of lament

Mourning and grief are widely recognized stages in processing trauma. Externalizing traumatic experience and the feelings associated with trauma can work towards removing shame and stigma. Lament, particularly biblical lament, helps provide language to those who may struggle to verbalize traumatic experience. Lament can also have nonverbal expressions through the use of visual art, music, and movement that can help communities process trauma. The language of lament can help survivors "express their truth." Practicing lament corporately provides a sense of thick support and validation.

Celebratory benefits of lament

Lament helps keep expressions of thanksgiving, celebration, and praise honest. Psalm 30 offers thanksgiving to God for healing and salvation from verge of death. However, we can see remnants of the lament that was surely prayed amid illness:

> To you, O LORD, I cried,
>   and to the LORD I made supplication:
> "What profit is there in my death,
>   if I go down to the Pit?
> Will the dust praise you?
>   Will it tell of your faithfulness?
> Hear, O LORD, and be gracious to me!
>   O LORD, be my helper!"
> (Psalm 30:8–10)

The psalm captures a vital dynamic of faith and relationship with the living God who helps, who goes down to the Pit. The psalmist's lament sets the stage for powerful praise,

> You have turned my mourning into dancing;
>   you have taken off my sackcloth
>   and clothed me with joy,
> so that my soul may praise you and not be silent.
>   O LORD my God, I will give thanks to you forever.
> (Psalm 30:11–12)

Empowering benefits of lament

Lament has the potential to destabilize unjust power systems as those who are wronged and suffering take their complaints directly to God, completely bypassing systems that are oriented around maintaining the status quo.[50] Lament can feel dangerous and subversive. It can engender complex emotions among worship participants as both catharsis and truth-telling, but also trigger deep resistance, denial, and hostility. These feelings can represent an experience of clean pain.

Hopeful benefits of lament

Hope is a powerful reservoir for resilience. It is more of a practice or action than an emotion and it is something that can be practiced on behalf of another during seasons when a person or community may be immobilized by crisis or tragedy. The act of lament is, at its core, deeply hopeful because it holds that life doesn't need to be this way, change is possible, and we have a God who cares and acts. Lament is life-affirming and thus can be a tool for building hope in congregations.

LAMENT AS A PRACTICE

While nothing we do or don't do in worship limits God's ability and power to reach God's people, especially in times of deep need, congregations can do more when it comes to expressing lament. As John Witvliet puts it, "*Everything* we do in church shapes how participants imagine God and God's ways with us."[51] Walter Brueggemann names this as "world forming."[52] The form that lament takes in collective settings helps to shape community theology and relationships. Leaders should be intentional about how and when lament is used for worship and other activities. The addition of lament to our worship services will not only offer a means of processing trauma, but also enrich our experience of other aspects of worship such as thanksgiving and praise.[53]

Studying lament and preaching *about* lament may be a good first step towards introducing the practice in a congregation. Helping people understand the background out of which biblical laments occurred and discussing the traumatic origins of much of the Bible can demystify and reveal how lament as a potent tool of faith and means of connection to God and God's loving power has always undergirded our faith.

Creating space for lament

Among other things, trauma-aware spaces are marked by choices, shared power, transparency, pacing that allows for processing and rest, authentic inclusion, and adaptability.[54] A space that is conducive for lament will want to consider these elements. Lament necessitates vulnerability—more vulnerability than the average churchgoer might feel comfortable sharing. Leaders will benefit from intentionality and care in incorporating lament into congregational life.

Experiment with smaller groups

It may be helpful to initially experiment with lament in smaller groups. Church members may form a small group to specifically focus on practices of lament. Leaders of existing groups may offer time for lament in Bible studies or prayer groups. Clergy may pray and discuss a psalm of lament with a church board or committee as part of a devotional time before a meeting. Clergy may pray a lament prayer as part of a staff meeting.

Bible translator June Dickie explored Psalm 55 with two small groups in Capricorn, an economically poor township of Cape Town, South Africa. The first group was a very small support group of young women fighting drug addiction and the second was a larger Bible study group of men and women. Dickie found that participants resonated with both "complaints" and "affirmations of trust," with those who had survived trauma identifying most with the laments.[55] Leaders may want to explore using different translations or paraphrases of the text with groups. The semantic range represented by different versions may offer new points of connection.

Try online space

Creating an online synchronous or asynchronous gathering space for lament can help participants feel safe and create greater access to a community where lament is encouraged. Post a video or instructions along with examples of how to write a lament prayer after the style of the Psalms. Allow people to post their own prayers of lament with names or anonymously. In seminary classes, I have invited students to post "six-word pandemic memoirs."[56] (For more on this process, see chapter 3, on storytelling.) Keeping it short makes it an accessible medium for expressing lament.

Incorporating lament into regular prayer life

One of the effects of trauma can be a reduced sense of curiosity and inability to engage in an activity that involves risk or creative energy. From an evolutionary standpoint, this seems reasonable. If a zebra has been chased by lions in the recent past, it will be less likely to venture out from protective cover. A stressed zebra is not a curious zebra.

Individuals and groups can suffer from some of the same effects of stress. Individuals can acknowledge and honor this stress within themselves if they experience internal resistance toward a new prayer practice. Leaders will want to take care with introducing a new practice with a stressed congregation. It may be easiest to incorporate elements of lament in ways that are already familiar and comfortable.

Prayer is our mother tongue of faith. Regardless of complex social dynamics and context, prayer is first and foremost connection with God. Prayer is a language between God and people, so it works with us, our tendencies, gifts, challenges, and limitations. Any perceived limitations on our part are not a limitation for communicating with God. Prayer can be visual, musical, and physical as well as spoken or written words.

Lament follows a distinct although flexible form that invites honesty about experiences of trauma, pain, injustice, and loss. In worship and other congregational gatherings, we can be creative about using a variety of means for people to express lament. Because one of the results of trauma is difficulty in speaking directly about the experience, using biblical language, body movement, visual art, and music can all provide a means of lamenting when the pain in unspeakable.

One congregation has a regular prayer practice that incorporates visual symbol and movement when the prayer is beyond words. Each bench in the worship space has a small basket of stones. During the prayers of the people following the sermon, prayers are offered on behalf of members and other broader concerns. Those who have a prayer that cannot be spoken are invited to place a stone on the communion table. Choosing a stone, walking to the front, and placing it are a form of prayer-in-action. The visual element helps others to also lift these unspoken concerns to God.

Following the horrible and tragic invasion of Ukraine by Russia in early 2022, pastor Brian Maguire created a prayer of lament that he shared with his congregation during his regular mid-week email reflection. This prayer of lament may have been new, but the context was familiar, and by using email, members could prayer the pray themselves. Readers might take the time, even now, to read this prayer out loud:

God of the suffering and the forgotten, God of fearful and fleeing,

God of the Cross

You never employed empires and armies but make yourself known in the most humble moments of gentle care.
You know that history is not drawn on maps, but in the interwoven tapestry of peoples' hearts.

We go about our daily lives and complain about the price of fuel.

And a little girl hurriedly packs a single suitcase for a lifetime.

An old man gets lost in the panicked crowds of the train station.

A dog sniffs at the bowl in its yard to which its owners will never return.

Fear begins to creep over the city like a cold damp stain blotting out life as hatred vies with terror for supremacy.

Let loose your better angels O Lord. Shield and guide your people who pray more fervently than we can imagine in our secure rest.

Show yourself now in word and deed. In miracles and the mundane.

Rouse up your heroes and stir the hearts of the multitude so your Kingdom may be manifest amid the wrack and ruin of our vanities.

Remind leaders everywhere that they stand under your judgment for eternity.

And most of all, remember the one we forget, the one of no account, the one without money, fame, or followers, who runs into the night alone and afraid.

You know your child by name even when we do not.

Save your child O God from the scourge of war let loose by evil men.

All our hopes and all our ends lie in you, your light shines still, even in the darkness. Amen.[57]

Praying the Psalms

In preaching and Bible study, it can be helpful to name and acknowledge the specific context from which biblical laments emerged and to highlight the circumstances which helped shape these words. However, in worship we regularly allow the language of scripture to become our words too. In faith we share a sense of unity with other believers across time and geography. A pastor friend reminds me that when we pray the Psalms we pray with the cloud of witnesses, two hundred generations of believers. While bringing voice to experience can be healing for trauma survivors, part of trauma's impact on the brain can impede the connection between experience and language. Allowing lament psalms to become "our" lament can be helpful.

June Dickie names several benefits in using lament psalms to process trauma in ministry. (1) Lament psalms provide a means of connection to others who suffer throughout time and in the present. Praying lament psalms in public worship validates and creates a container of safety for deep emotions. (2) Lament psalms provide language for what people struggle to express. Lament psalms convey anger and agony; they often cast blame on perpetrators and call upon God to act. Lament psalms use general language that can allow us to bring our world to the text and encourage us to offer bold and fierce prayers. (3) Lament psalms as poetry are a particularly evocative art form for processing trauma. Poetry does not necessitate "coherence and closure."[58]

Psalms of lament can be used as an opportunity for prayer and reflection. A lament psalm can be spoken together or divided into parts for leaders and other worshipers. A lament psalm can be spoken by one voice while others pray or reflect silently.

Augustine is often quoted as likening singing in worship to "praying twice."[59] Psalms can be sung with potentially greater benefits for nurturing a sense of community, solidarity, and processing trauma. Singing is beneficial for trauma survivors as it taps into the right side of the brain.[60] The left side of the brain is often more incapacitated in traumatic response. Singing offers a much-needed right-brain outlet. Singing together also generates a sense of being together physically. Breathing together and blending voices together generates a complex sense of awareness of others that helps to soothe, regulate, and synchronize nervous systems. Congregations can sing psalms together or broken up with a leader or cantor and congregational refrain.

Along with singing, movement may also help psalms of lament unlock areas of stress and grief in bodies. Simple motions such as making and releasing a fist or turning palms to face upward or standing to speak connect more deeply than saying words alone.

Most lament psalms convey depths of pain as well as offering thanks to God and naming hope. This resonates with a nondualistic approach to life after trauma. The experience of trauma is not erased even while life continues. People can experience beauty and meaning alongside pain and loss. The resurrected Christ still had wounds from the trauma of the cross. These wounds were not the only operating feature of his identity, although they did provide a means for his disciples to connect with him.[61]

Creating your own lament prayer

Studying lament prayers in scripture reveals a common structure that can help people voice their own specific prayers of lament. Working generally with the structure "address to God, complaint(s), confession of trust, petition and sometimes a vow of praise," June Dickie has conducted lament workshops with groups that studied and discussed Psalms 3 and 13 as part of preparing to create their own prayers. Dickie notes key observations that participants lifted from the text, such as the "boldness" of the psalmists, the "raw honest emotion," the requests for God to intervene and the "glimpses of hope" within the psalms.[62]

Offering individuals or groups a set of prompts or questions can help with creating a present-day prayer of lament that feels authentic and resonant with the situation at hand. Dickie suggests that participants steer away from "churchy" words or language in their responses.[63] Here is a suggested list of questions that follows the basic structure outlined above:[64]

1. What names do you use for God; how do you feel most comfortable speaking to the Divine?

2. What is your complaint? What is bothering you? What hurts? Where is the pain in your life, in our world?

3. What specifically do you long for God to do for you, for others, for the world?

4. Where is justice needed? How can God level the scales and uplift those who have been on the receiving end of sin and brokenness? How do you need God to bring vindication through dealing directly with individuals, groups, or systems that have caused harm?

5. How has God been present to you in the past? What do you know about who God is? How does God give you hope in the present?

6. Imagine God's justice, comfort, power, love, and
    presence. Imagine God as a mother lion and you
    as her cub; imagine tender care and fierce defense.
    Recall Jesus' actions of healing, feeding, listening,
    questioning assumptions, and teaching new ways. If
    you have the words, feel free to share words of praise
    or thankfulness.

A dynamic exists between those whose lives are "in balance" and those whose lives are "out of balance."[65] Those whose lives are currently in balance may be so invested in the status quo that they are afraid of God's intervention on behalf of others. Leaders may gently remind that the realm of God isn't marked by finite resources, that one's own dignity, justice, love, and health are not diminished when extended to others. Rather, as Martin Luther King Jr. famously noted, "Injustice anywhere is a threat to justice everywhere."[66]

Because of concerns with power imbalances, when working with a group to create a corporate lament, it may work best for the group to have similar concerns, such as a support group of people recovering from addiction, a grief support group, a group for people dealing with infertility, a group for families supporting those with mental illness, a group of people without permanent addresses. Using a lament prayer written by a small group lifts this perspective to others in worship who can bear witness. It validates the perspective of potentially marginalized groups and in a sense participates in the justice that the lament is seeking.

LAMENT AS ELEMENTS OF THE WORSHIP SERVICE

Lament can be incorporated into nearly every aspect of worship, not only for special services but as part of regular worship. In the case of services entirely focused on lament, each movement of the service can be shaped with attention to lament. For typical Sunday services, confession, music, preaching, prayers of the people, poetry, ritual, and children's activities can all provide an opportunity to incorporate lament. These elements are discussed in turn below.

It may be beneficial for congregations to experiment with lament as a special element in worship or as a focus for special services. The Calvin Institute of Christian Worship offers a service of lament based on Psalm 13. Authors note the importance of taking care with the elements of the service when designing worship around lament. Setting a tone in the call to worship is important, as are the invitation to hear the Word and respond, and the benediction or sending. The institute's service uses *The Message* to offer a more contemporary paraphrase of Psalm 13. The congregational prayer is a prayer of lament, situated as a response to the sermon. This prayer of lament is constructed for four voices, with the congregation singing the Taizé refrain "O Lord, hear my prayer." Sections of the prayer loosely follow the structure of a lament psalm: addressing God, expressing pain and discouragement, interceding for specific needs, affirming faith in God.[67]

The benediction can benefit from special attention in a service of lament and function as "seal" on the service and a vehicle for God's promise to go with us.

A congregation may also wish to hold a vigil following a stressful, violent, or traumatic event with larger implications. Elements of lament may be present in these special services as well. Planners will need to consider the scope of who may be present. What constituent groups should be invited? If the vigil is intended to be interfaith or not expressly Christian, other faith leaders may need to be invited to assist. Including a ritual that allows participants to voice a lament in a style that is authentic to them and allows for a range of responses may take the place of a formal lament.

Lament need not be saved for a separate service. Leaders can incorporate lament as a practice into nearly every element of a typical Sunday service. Many worship services follow the traditional *ordo*, which is biblical and deeply relational in structure.

- Gathering
- Word
- Response
- Sending

Elements of worship find home within this structure depending on the congregation, the season, and the occasion.

Celebration is a vital element of much preaching in the Black church. Celebration is highly emotive, dynamic, and participatory—an experience of the gospel here and now. Luke Powery, dean of Duke Chapel, pairs lament with celebration in worship.[68] This pairing addresses our eschatological situation, because the way of faith in our world still passes by the cross. Our world is also touched by resurrection, and all of creation is pulled toward the promise of redemption. Hence the need to complement lament with celebration and praise for what God has done, is doing, and will do among us. Lament can become part of the everyday language of the church alongside celebration so that it is always one of the tools at our disposal.

Leaders can incorporate services of lament linked to collective suffering in our world in situations and seasons of the Christian year where the Christian life opens natural space for such acknowledgments. Good Friday is a natural place for

lament. Jesus' lament from the cross could be expanded in a
sermon to include present-day laments.

With a full acknowledgment of suffering and death on
Good Friday, the defiant cry of Easter before the open grave
sounds true and powerful. The defiance of Easter carries
through to funeral services that not only make space for deep
grief and loss but also bear witness to our deepest belief that
Jesus has truly defeated death. When we sing an Easter hymn
at a funeral, it can feel cathartic; like shaking our collective
fist at death.

Lament and confession

Confession in public worship makes an existential statement
about humanity's relationship to God. When we confess, we
acknowledge our inability and brokenness in the presence of
God's love and merciful power. Lament can sometimes feel
like a cousin to the practice of confession. When congregations confess, there are often individual elements such as a
pause where individuals can confess their own sins, and corporate elements where we confess our collective sin. Often the
focus in confession is acknowledgment of active wrongdoing
or being complicit in wrongdoing.

With so much focus on "sinners," the perspective of the
"sinned against" is often missing. Lament can provide an outlet that acknowledges sin from another perspective, a perspective that calls on God to intervene amid sin, not only as divine
pardoner and one who transforms sinners, but as one who
saves and heals the sinned-against and who disrupts circumstances from which sin emerges.

Congregations who regularly confess in worship can experiment with substituting a prayer of lament or adding a prayer
of lament to the prayer of confession. Congregations who do

not regularly include a confession can consider incorporating a prayer of lament during a particular season or as part of a worship series.

Congregations who include confession in communion liturgies but have some flexibility about the form of the liturgy may consider adding a prayer of lament. Lament in the context of communion acknowledges the wrongs in the world that God has promised to set right. The celebration of communion represents a place where the justice of the realm of God meets us here and now.

Musical lament

Music carries the potential to connect to brains under stress in ways that spoken word cannot. Singing creates a sense of connection and support as participants breathe and blend voices together. In addition to sung prayers or musical arrangements of the Psalms, any song that speaks about distress and suffering in a frank way may be incorporated into a lament. Contemporary songs such as Matt Redman's "Blessed Be Your Name" or Mark A. Miller's "Lament: My Heart is Breaking" (lyrics by Adam Tice) and "I Choose Love" (lyrics by Lindy Thompson) could work as part of a congregational lament. The meditative structure of music from the Taizé Community can allow for reflection or create a participatory support for ritual action.

Spirituals are one of the strongest musical forms of lament. The spirituals as a family of song connect deeply to the complex biblical understanding of lament as expressing anguish and protest, and as a call for action to God and the witnessing community. One cannot separate the spirituals from the horrific cauldron of slavery from which they emerged. The spirituals testify to life and humanity amidst a death-dealing and profoundly inhuman institution.

The spirituals emerged from real people having real experiences, so congregations may want to include an introduction or prayer honoring suffering and loss by enslaved African Americans. We want to avoid contributing to violence that forgets or thoughtlessly appropriates another's pain or collapses it into our own. Remembering those who first voiced these musical laments invites them into our midst.

Laments in the spirituals call across the generations and continue to hold us accountable. The words of the spirituals are a witness calling the continued actions and culture of white supremacy into account. We may find ourselves among those who must repent and change behavior.

Among others, widely known spirituals that may lend themselves to a lament orientation in worship include "Kumbaya, My Lord," "Didn't My Lord Deliver Daniel," "Sometimes I Feel Like a Motherless Child," "Do Lord Remember Me," and "I Want Jesus to Walk with Me." Spirituals may be interspersed with spoken prayers or hummed by the congregation while one voice laments on behalf of the whole congregation.

Lament in the sermon

Preaching that is informed by the complexity of biblical lament is preaching normed by the complexity of the human situation. We stand between the cross and the resurrection, using what professor of homiletics and liturgics James Kay refers to as bifocal vision. Bifocal vision sees need and suffering in our world as well as the dawning realm of God, the presence of God, and the pull of God's realized and still coming promises that give us strength and hope.[69]

Luke Powery describes six marks of sermonic lament.[70]

1. Sermonic lament includes concrete expression of human pain. Pain can be individual or collective, with a variety of

manifestations. Preachers may want to track whether they tend to focus on individual or collective suffering over time to achieve a balance in preaching. Individual concerns and issues often have social manifestation, and trauma experiences between individuals and larger structures are connected. A particular story or concrete example unlocks the imaginations of listeners more effectively than generalizations. A goal in preaching that incorporates lament is to equip active participation by listeners so they might see connections in their own lives and contexts, even if details differ.

2. Another mark of lament is imperative, direct language. Direct speech towards God in the presence of a witnessing community shows that the church need not shy away from speaking into the most difficult aspects of human life.

3. Lament in preaching uses "we" language to include the preacher in solidarity with the suffering and acknowledge our own complicity in the occasion of lament.

4. Biblical lament is rooted in deep faith. Sermons that incorporate aspects of lament will also profess belief in God even during struggle. Theologically, we turn towards the resurrection even while naming the pain of crucifixion still unfolding in our world.

5. Part of lament involves calling for God to act as God has done in the past, which means consciously recalling past situations where God intervened. Preaching lament also involves celebrating resurrection and God's activity among us. No traumatic event is beyond the care and healing of God. Remembering past divine acts and naming God's action in the present can help restore or reinforce a sense of identity as "God's own people" to a community. Hope is a muscle that gets stronger as it is flexed. Lament preaching flexes the muscle of hope.

6. Finally, preaching marked by lament involves "heightened, passionate rhetoric." What serves as "heightened and passionate" is highly contextual, but preachers will want to dial up elements of emotive qualities and speech performance to show listeners that this is important. For example, using direct address communicates God's presence in a more intimate but heightened way. "God says to you—nothing is beyond my love, no hole is too deep for me to follow." Or God says, "I love you, you are my own precious child." Singing, speaking in higher, more playful tones, or more loudly or more quietly than normal, or varying the pace so that the preaching is significantly slower or quicker than the typical pacing signals a sense of heightened energy and passion.

The distinctive shape of biblical laments that move from plea to praise can be reflected in the structure of a sermon.[71] Professor of homiletics Paul Scott Wilson's "four page" theological grammar, which focuses on divine action in the biblical text and in our world, moves from trouble to grace. Preachers name the trouble in the text, analogous trouble in our world, God's action (grace) in the text, and finally God's action (grace) in our world.[72]

Professor of preaching and worship Sally Brown categorizes sermonic laments by the accent that emerges in preaching. These postures give pastors choices for embracing lament that honor the particularities of the needs and situation of a congregation. *Pastoral* laments will focus on validating a present experience of suffering, grief, and disorientation by crying out to God for help. *Critical prophetic* laments protest, decry injustice, and invite critical self-examination. Finally, a *theological-interrogatory* approach to preaching lament asks challenging theological questions and explores the nature of God.[73]

Preaching can also support lament by validating lament expressions that we see in our world. Naming silence, questioning, the holler, and expressions of fear and rage that we experience in our world as implicit prayers of lament can help us begin to process trauma and suffering that inspire these responses.

Lament and the prayers of the people

Perhaps one of the most natural places to include a lament in many worship services is within the prayers of the people. Newly written prayers can be punctuated with "kyrie eleison" or lines from a lament psalm, corporately sung or spoken. In prayers of the people, lament pairs well with intercession on behalf of those who are suffering in our world.

Poetry as a language of lament

When working with pastors or church groups, I often use poetry as an entry point to conversation and connection. New or established poems can also be utilized in worship. As an art form, poetry serves as metaphorical speech that signals to more than what each word represents. Creating poetry has been helpful to survivors of trauma. Poetry in worship is more about experience than explanation. Hymn lyrics are poetry and can be read as such in worship to call attention to the words and the worlds they reveal. However, because the language is so evocative, worship leaders will want to take care that the poetry doesn't harmfully trigger some listeners.

Lament as ritual

Words often fail to express the experience of trauma. Ritual can provide means of physically releasing stress and expressing pain in nonverbal ways. Rituals can complement spoken lament and allow for wider participation in a congregation.

A visual artist at Hamilton Mennonite Church in Ontario led a ritual for the congregation's yearly observance of Toten Sontag, an observance in the Russian Mennonite congregation that acknowledges the loss of loved ones, somewhat like All Saints observances in other traditions. Seating was arranged in the round, with a large bare tree branch planted in a pot. Worshipers were invited to take strips of cloth. Later in the service the cloth was tied or draped to the tree as a visual sign of remembrance.

Rituals don't need to be complex or original to be meaningful. Inviting members to bring a memento connected to a traumatic event, kneeling, lighting candles, or brainstorming an act of compassionate witness can all contribute to a sense of expressing lament.

Lament and children

Amid pandemic restrictions, disappointments, and loss, my seven-year-old daughter Maggie decided to plant seeds indoors.[74] "The season is wrong" I told her. "We won't be able to transplant them outside." Nevertheless, she planted sunflowers in a small pot, diligently watering it until small shoots sprung up. Concerned about the growing plants getting light as the days grew shorter, she moved the pot to her windowsill. She would video chat to her best friend daily to show her the progress of the seeds which had by this time put out small leaves. She proudly reported the seeds' progress over the phone to her grandparents. This growing project was such a source of joy when many other activities were canceled, and opportunities restricted.

We don't know what happened—it might have been gravity or our dog being curious, but one morning we woke up to an anguished wail. Running to her bedroom we found her kneeling on the floor. The small pot had fallen off the sill, dirt was scattered, and the little plants were broken. "Why?" she asked through tears. It was a primal question—a question rooted deeper than answers we could offer. I can't recall what I said, probably along the lines of "Sometimes these things just happen."

My daughter's question was a lament. A lament for her little plants but also likely for other things that had been lost and disrupted. Questions are common responses to traumatic experience. Not only "Why?" but "Could this have been stopped?" and "Is this someone's fault?" Encouraging questions and claiming these as a means of lament frees us from having to answer these usually unanswerable questions. As a form of lament, they can stand on their own.

Questions directed to God may seem to threaten God's power or signal a weakness in faith. In truth, questions directed to God signal a strong faith, a belief that God can take on these questions, that God is in dynamic relationship with us. Questions may be a particularly beneficial way to help children (and adults) express lament.

Children and teens in the church are not exempt from individual and collective trauma. Young people grapple with many of the resulting signs of "acting in" and "acting out" that can result from unaddressed trauma, loss, and grief. Doctors have documented an increase in eating disorders and other mental illnesses during the COVID-19 pandemic, particularly among children who were already vulnerable or dealing with challenges.[75] Overburdened healthcare providers have not always been able to provide young people or their families the support they need. The kids are not okay.

Church leaders cannot substitute for professional mental and physical healthcare, but they can help. Pastors can destigmatize and validate the need for support. Pastors can support caregivers as they advocate for what children and teenagers need. Other youth and children can also support in appropriate ways. When I was a youth pastor many years ago, one of the teens in the periphery of the group spent weeks in a facility in treatment for addiction. The youth group wrote letters and sent care packages, which forged a stronger connection to church when the teen came home. Helping support and show love to their friend also affirmed the agency of the youth group members.

Too often the losses that young people may experience are minimized. Adults consider the loss of prom or a sports season trivial compared to loss of life. Churches too are largely driven by the goals and beliefs of adult members. Children and teenagers may be cherished but not given agency or fully validated in their experiences. Youth-oriented worship services are often dominated by praise songs that don't express the full complexity of human experiences or provide nuanced theological tools or language. Lament can offer additional language and access to relationship with God in a way that may feel more authentic for youth struggling with grief, loss, anger, and stress.

It is important to acknowledge the weight of accumulated loss and stress for all members of the church. Lament can provide an outlet for losses large and small. Children and teens can participate in larger congregational lament practices or engage in lament in smaller Sunday school groups or during children's worship. As with adults, some explanation will help them better understand how lament functions as a prayer. The unique needs of different developmental stages may mean that leaders need to be especially concrete with what children lament.

Leaders may be able to incorporate lament prayers created by children and youth into broader worship and congregational gatherings. It may also be helpful to create a resource about lament that could be used by families at home. Such a resource could include a guide to writing a lament prayer based on psalms of lament and tools for a simple ritual such as creating a candleholder for a battery-operated candle to call attention to God's listening and helping presence among us when we pray.

*   *   *

Responding to pain and injustice is instinctual and deeply human. The wisdom of our ancestors of faith echoes through scripture, offering a full spectrum of human emotions and responses to experiences joyful, agonizing, celebratory, and traumatic. The presence of lament in scripture is deeply validating for all who suffer and experience injustice. Lament empowers those who lack power, whose backs are up against the wall. Lament takes human anguish directly to God, and calls upon God to see and respond, to live up to God's good promises.

For individuals and communities today, lament can be a vital, prayerful practice that has potential to process trauma and facilitate healing and resilience. And yet lament is underutilized and not fully understood by many believers. Leaders can teach about lament and use lament in various congregational settings with young children up to the most senior church members. Lament is spiritually and bodily beneficial, offering validation, empowerment, and liberation from captivity to broken systems. When we are broken, angry, and at a loss for words, we can allow our ancestors of faith to speak for us. Praying psalms of lament provides us language and buoys us with the faith of generations of believers who walk this way with us.

THREE

Storytelling

In my preaching classes, I regularly give a lecture that discusses types of illustrations that can be useful in a sermon. The lecture culminates with a focus on stories. Stories are ideal for preaching because they allow something small and particular to serve as an entry point into something larger. The details and elements of stories elicit responses and resonance with listeners, inviting them to participate in making meaning from what they are hearing, to make connections to their own lives. Stories can shape our understandings of identity and purpose. Stories from our world that bear witness to the gospel are key ingredients in sermons that nurture faith and encourage hope and resilience.

In a polarized political climate, stories can also seem like tinder for fires of division that may be smoldering in communities and congregations. When a Tennessee school board banned Art Spiegelman's graphic novel about the Nazi Holocaust, sales of the book spiked and both social and traditional media outlets exploded with opinions.[1] This is only the latest skirmish in public schools concerning how and whose history is taught. In my own local school district, anxiety focused on critical race theory and how gender identity is discussed at school caused some tense letters to the editor and a contentious school board battle.

Disputes over how to tell the story of human history are not new. On a recent podcast, author and historian Tamim Ansary described historical events as bricks and beams, and narrative as the tool that turns them into something coherent like a cathedral.[2]

We live in a time when many formerly accepted narratives of history are rightly being dismantled. Events are being pried loose, and our cultural "cathedrals" are crashing down. Deconstruction can be healing when it uncovers buried truths and validates those whose stories have been hidden. But the loss of common narratives and agreed-upon understanding of our own past can also be destabilizing, painful, and scary.

Trauma serves as its own kind of wrecking ball to the narrative cathedrals we construct in our own lives and communities. Trauma dismantles narrative threads that give life meaning, destroys coherence, and understandably calls identity, relationships, and purpose into question. In the heartbreaking travelogue *The Shadow of Imana: Travels in the Heart of Rwanda*, artist Véronique Tadjo describes the traumatized state of an entire culture that struggles to engage with the enormity and horror of the aftermath of the Rwandan genocide of 1994. Her perspective is important, as her descriptions and reflections offer us a set of lenses to bear witness to humanity unraveled. The book is a stream of particularities and observations, a mix of some narrative elements but lacking an overarching narrative whole. All the people and places in her book have been deeply impacted by the trauma of genocide. In one part of her book, she describes how individual bodies were exhumed from mass graves, identified, and examined closely as examples standing in for the larger whole.[3] The places she visits and the diverse people she meets similarly serve as stand-ins for a larger whole. This is part of the gift of storytelling.

Finding ways to make meaning in the aftermath of trauma is a vital part of processing for many. This doesn't mean that survivors need to recount painful traumatic events—this can re-trigger and entrench corrosive stress responses. Pastors and church leaders without mental health training and certification are not qualified to engage in narrative therapy techniques.

Narrative has a powerful gravitational force on collective identity. This chapter is purposeful and thoughtful about ways to harness narrative's power. Thoughtful storytelling can draw a community together following trauma and help people make meaning and move forward. Stories remind us of what is important, what we deeply cherish, and what we want to preserve. In the aftermath of trauma when so much is up in the air, storytelling can be a grounding and orienting practice.

However, *story is not sacred*. Storytelling has its limits, particularly in the wake of trauma. Trauma defies a simple clear narrative structure. We need look no further than the ways our global struggle with COVID-19 has defied the early narratives. In late 2020, when all hope focused on a vaccine, no one would have guessed that more than two years later hundreds of Americans would still be dying of COVID daily. How does one process when we have no idea how an experience will end?

This chapter explores the practice of storytelling as a means to process collective trauma. I discuss how narrative functions in relationship to collective identity, memory, and purpose. I focus on parables as a form of biblical storytelling and address the need for careful discernment amidst many powerful cultural narratives. The final sections offer ideas for preachers and worship leaders to harness the power of story and facilitate storytelling to help metabolize traumatic experiences.

It is not "any" story that we as Christians claim as redemptive. The story of salvation, the movement from enslavement to promised land and from cross to resurrection, is the most vital story that shapes Christian identity and community. Indeed, this is the storied identity into which we are baptized. And yet we cannot grasp sacred story completely—rather, it grasps us. Professor of philosophy Stephen Crites describes it as "awakening to a sacred story."[4]

STORY AND HUMAN EXPERIENCE

As long as people have existed, we have told stories. Storytelling appears throughout various cultures although the format and practice may differ. In his essay "The Narrative Quality of Human Experience," Stephen Crites highlights what we implicitly know to be true. The way we make sense of or process experiences through time is narrative.[5] Families tell stories for many reasons: passing along core beliefs, explaining circumstances, and helping to generate a sense of closeness, belonging, and identity, among others. I have fond memories of my daughter telling me about her day when she was in preschool, a breathless string of events: "And then we had circle time, and then we played in the gym, and then we had snack." My mother and grandfather are also storytellers. They have recently taken to writing down memories and family stories. These were especially precious during the early days of the pandemic when we were unable to be together physically.

My family's Mennonite tradition has gathered core stories, collectively preserving important elements of testimony and identity dating from when the early Anabaptists were experiencing intense persecution and threat. *The Martyrs Mirror* is a volume bearing witness to the faithful lives and resulting death of early Christians starting with the apostles and moving forward to recount the martyrdom of many Anabaptists. The illustrations printed from wood carvings help lodge the stories in readers' imaginations. This hefty tome was once a mainstay of many Mennonite family or congregational bookshelves. My brothers and I loved to read the stories as children. My husband and I were given one as a wedding gift! Only relatively recently are Mennonite communities grappling in a more critical way with the legacy and formative power of these core stories of martyrdom and how they continue to shape Mennonite identity and practice.

We all have our own backgrounds and traditions that are passed on, in large part, by stories. There are many reasons why stories are not shared or might be shifted or even fabricated. In an interview with adoptee and writer Nicole Chung, historian Kate Bowler mused that families sometimes "tell the stories they can bear to tell."[6] This is especially true when families have stories of deep pain and trauma. Those who shift family stories to make them more bearable do so from a place of deep kindness and care, although subsequent generations often experience the pain of unaddressed trauma without understanding why.

Storytelling can be especially important for processing trauma. Psychiatrist Judith Herman names three distinct stages in moving forward after trauma: "establishing safety, reconstructing the trauma story, and restoring the connection between survivors and their community."[7] Storytelling can be useful as a tool in stages two and three. Storytelling can restore agency to survivors as they remember and grieve what happened, shape memory, and share their own story. Storytelling can destigmatize causes of trauma, establish connections with other survivors, help people make meaning of life after trauma, and mobilize communities to change systems that contribute to trauma in our world.

STORYTELLING IN SCRIPTURE

The Bible tells us the story of our faith through the words and witness of generations of faithful Jewish and early Christian believers. The stories in the Bible form our identity as God's people and show us how to live as disciples of Jesus. In the aftermath of trauma, scriptural stories, particularly stories that place a range of human experience within God's care, and stories that testify to the life, death, and resurrection of Jesus can be healing and restorative.

The image of "Jesus the storyteller" teaching in parables may be lodged in many of our imaginations. We may picture him seated outside with his robe hitched up, hands gesturing, face expressive, showing intent listeners and passersby a glimpse of the realm of God through ordinary stuff in our world: seeds, family dynamics, unexpected tragedy, and unexpected kindness. Jesus telling parables is a powerful affirmation of the blessing of incarnation and God's deep love for the "ordinary stuff" of our world. Indeed, the presence of God regularly makes ordinary stuff sacred in worship. This view can baptize and bless our own storytelling for furthering God's healing work in our midst.

New Testament scholar Amy-Jill Levine counts us modern-day listeners to Jesus' parables as fortunate that Jesus' private explanations of the parables are mostly absent from the Gospels. Jesus' teaching in parables places us in the crowd of those gathered to hear him and those who are left to grapple with these potent stories, and the richness of meaning that can often change and adapt to speak to us in a variety of situations and circumstances. The surplus of meaning found in stories also leaves space for misunderstanding. Scripture tells us that Jesus' own disciples frequently failed to catch the meaning of his parables.[8]

Levine writes about the words of challenge imbedded in Jesus' stories and the loss of the "art of listening" that helps us hear the challenge and hold the range of meaning without taking the easiest and most well-worn interpretive pathways.[9] She helpfully steers us away from focusing on what a parable means and toward what a parable "does." Such an approach is fertile for trauma-aware ministry, where a range of possibilities opened by a parable may gently invite diverse worshipers to join us in all their particularity on the interpretive journey and find themselves transformed and changed.

Parables span both the Old Testament and New Testament and would have been a familiar form of discourse. The communication approaches represented by a parable are as much about the imaginative and polyvalent power of metaphor or simile as they are about the focused thrust of narrative. The best stories are also able to capture tensive possibility. When Jesus says "The kingdom of heaven is like . . . ," our imaginations are sparked to make connections.

When studying a parable, it may be helpful to create a list that opens interpretive possibilities. In Matthew 13:45–46, for example, Jesus shares a brief parable about a pearl. The text says, "The kingdom of heaven is like a merchant in search of fine pearls; on finding one pearl of great value, he went and sold all that he had and bought it." With Levine's reminder that parables are meant to challenge listeners among other aims, here are some possible connections between a valuable pearl and the "kingdom of heaven," or realm of God.

- The realm of God is deeply discerning, seeking only the finest.
- Size is not a measure of value in the realm of God.
- The realm of God is worth all that we have.
- Maybe believers are the merchant and Jesus is the pearl.
- Maybe we are the pearl and Jesus is the merchant.
- Pearls are created by an irritant in the oyster. Is pain involved in the journey to the realm of God, and what are possible connections to the cross?
- Pearls were rare in the ancient world—many listeners would never have even seen one.
- Oysters are not kosher.
- Unlike precious gemstones, pearls are produced by a living creature.
- Pearls are beautiful but not necessarily "useful." How will the merchant live, having sold everything for a pearl?[10]
- How does the parable connect to the extravagant love of God that defies the world's logic?
- Pearls are tiny—and thus easily lost.
- As Levine cautions, the realm of God cannot be commodified. The realm of God is not a person or an object but is connected to seeking and transformation that happens upon discovery of the unexpected.

Making a list like this can help tap into a range of pathways opened by even a short parable. A parable can be a helpful teaching tool to open possibilities, to challenge and activate listeners, and to help them understand something that is vast and difficult. These features render parables as a generative model for how storytelling can help process traumatic experience.

While we may use story for a variety of reasons, in the wake of trauma, story may be an enticing way to "activate" congregations to imaginatively engage, to open, to find themselves and God's presence in a text and in our world, and to begin to find ways to process difficult experiences that defy language or logic.

TRAUMA AND STORYTELLING

For many individuals and communities, our sense of identity is implicitly shaped by the stories we have absorbed over the years. These implicit aspects of identity often are unexamined until something happens that contradicts what we thought we knew. Trauma creates a sense of rupture in that narrative quality of experience.

Traumatic experience resists the sense of resolution that many of us equate with storytelling. While children are routinely taught that a story needs to have a beginning, middle, and end, our sense of any of these elements are upended in the aftermath of trauma, particularly our sense of "end." Indeed, as the COVID-19 pandemic has progressed many have struggled to come to terms with living with a lack of closure or resolution with this intense source of suffering and stress. It has become clear that there will be no single moment when the virus is vanquished, no definitive ticker-tape parade for public health officials, and no shared singular moment when the mass of humanity worldwide can rush into the streets and embrace our neighbors, weeping with relief and joy. In my own household, our language around making plans has shifted from saying "After this is over . . ." to "After we are vaccinated . . ." to "We will see how things look."

Trauma changes identity

For many, traumatic experiences have severed connection to their past, to their family's own story. Descendants of enslaved

Americans of African descent often find it difficult to trace
their ancestors past the period of enslavement with certainty
because dehumanizing treatment and practices disregarded
relational bonds. A person who was adopted may grieve a lack
of connection or knowledge related to biological relatives.

A desire to learn more of one's own story to gain greater
understanding into present lives and relationships can motivate
someone to check out Ancestry.com or take a DNA test. Many
people who thought they knew their past discover secrets and
unknown parts of their story. A recent survey notes that over a
quarter of those who take a mail-in DNA test are surprised by
the discovery of an unknown close relative.[11] This kind of new
knowledge can turn your world upside down and rattle your
sense of identity and history.

In the program *Finding Your Roots*, Henry Louis Gates
guides celebrities, politicians, artists, and other public figures
through their own family histories, often revealing surprising
stories and facts that contradict what guests thought they
knew about themselves. These surprises sometimes offer new
insights and new stories that give an expanded and more complicated understanding of family and community of origin.

As noted in earlier chapters, collective trauma is profoundly
disorienting. Without familiar life landmarks, we may not
know who we are. Collective trauma shows us in a profound
way that we are not "special" or somehow immune from the
vulnerability of being human.[12]

An experience of collective or mass trauma can be compared to a strong hurricane hitting land. Grand Isle, Louisiana,
was unrecognizable following Hurricane Ida. High winds and
flooding changed the landscape. In aerial photographs, the
shape of the entire coastline looked different. With familiar
landmarks submerged or destroyed, even lifelong residents

can feel disoriented or lost—they don't recognize their own neighborhoods.

Loss of defining events, rituals, practices, and sacred or cherished physical spaces can disrupt a collective sense of who we are that is implicitly grounded in "what we have always done." My husband is a pastor of a small rural congregation with a history of loss, already struggling with declining membership and anxiety around change. COVID-19 robbed them of two deeply cherished aspects of identity; choir and an extended fellowship time after Sunday worship where members would talk and share a light meal together. For some, these two activities simply "were church"; without those places of connection, meaningful aspects of identity have been lost.

Other groups may struggle with concern around whose story is being told during an unfolding crisis. Not feeling heard or seen can lead to doubt. Congregations who met for worship with restrictions and drastic shifts in practice have had different experiences from congregations who stopped meeting face to face for an extended and open-ended period of time. During the height of pandemic restrictions, lay leadership was frequently sidelined or diminished. Without diversity in leadership, public worship may not reflect the diversity of the congregation. Church members may no longer "see themselves" reflected in the messages or practices coming from leaders.

Congregations have lost members and personnel, and have not had a chance to mourn and bear witness together. Whether because of COVID-19 or other causes, most congregations have been touched by death and loss without an opportunity to gather to memorialize or bear witness to resurrection hope. The seminary where I teach experienced the retirement of longtime and beloved staff members. Several congregations in my community have experienced pastor transitions. These losses change who we are and are made more difficult without a chance for a proper sending, blessing, or goodbye. Further, many community members have experienced loss on a personal level, which becomes part of shared grief.

Traumatic experiences can rattle a sense of basic trust in how the world works. In the midst of stress, loss, and grief, the way a congregation defines itself changes. Members feel "underwater" and look for familiar places to grip and hold. Basic narratives of self-understanding change. Trust in God looks different and feels difficult because so much is unfamiliar. As another example, the traumas of war and poverty drive many in our world to seek asylum in another country, where they are often faced with difficult legal processes, a different language, and new customs. In the words of the psalmist, "How could we possibly sing the LORD's song on foreign soil?" (Psalm 137:4 CEB).

Even "positive" changes in self-identity can be disorienting. Researchers Laurence Calhoun and Richard Tedeschi note that after coming through traumatic experience, survivors may view themselves as not only more vulnerable, fragile, and finite, but also stronger. The world may now be seen as more dangerous or capricious, but having survived, people can face the unknown with confidence and openness to taking on a new identity or role.[13] For example, the teenaged survivors of the Marjory Stoneman Douglas High School mass shooting became bold activists, founding a youth-led movement, March For Our Lives, and meeting directly with politicians and lobbyists to advocate for an end to gun violence.

Trauma limits our engagement with others' stories
Other people's stories are important—we understand who we are as we interact with others who are different from and

similar to us. God may use another person's story to touch our hearts and bring healing. This is part of the power of testimony. But over time, traumatic experiences erode our ability to engage with others. Trauma responses can turn off parts of the brain; we experience a fight-flight-freeze response. Trauma can impact our perception so that we may see the world in "all or nothing" or "us versus them" ways. We may lose our ability to flex, to listen to another person's story, to adapt, to appreciate nuance, and to experience grace and love through the stories of others.

In her TED talk, Nigerian novelist Chimamanda Ngozi Adichie names the danger in using primarily "one story" to define others.[14] Adichie recalls a childhood experience with a household employee who came from a poor family and her shock to learn that a member of this poor family had created a beautiful woven basket. She had only considered the family with her "one story" of poverty rather than a multifaceted story that included artistic talents and beauty. Years later when Adichie attended university in the United States, her roommate had only "one story" of the continent of Africa that focused on suffering and war. She struggled to understand the particularity of Adichie's actual life in Nigeria.

The nature of the pandemic has limited our ability to make and strengthen relationships in the periphery of our lives, to expand our perspectives beyond just "one story." In *The Atlantic*, Amanda Mull writes about the loss of whole categories of relationships. Casual relationships or weak ties have been lost, and serendipitous social encounters are rare and at certain times in the pandemic were impossible.[15] Without casual interactions, our perspective can become myopic and prone to "in-group processing" that creates "us versus them" thinking.

Congregations have also had to navigate the loss of relationships at the edges of community. If someone occasionally tunes into a YouTube broadcast of worship, they are unlikely to receive emails from the church office or be in direct contact with leadership. If an online listener encounters "one story" preaching that feels disconnected from their personal experience, follow-up conversation is unlikely. In fact, many listeners click away after mere minutes.

Congregations have also lost or limited story-expanding connections that happen with community events such as a rummage sale or community meal. If these events are continuing amidst the ebb and flow of infection rates, they are different, less broad, and likely have less space for direct human-to-human story-swapping.

Not only has external story-expansion suffered, relationships within communities are also affected by traumatic stress. Community identity is built on shared story, shared commitments, and shared practices. In his book on early Christian formation, Alan Kreider highlights the deep and dynamic connections between "belief, behavior, and belonging."[16] Our sense of connection is deeply linked to the dynamics of shared values and lifestyle choices.

Recent traumatic experiences have affected what we hold in common as communities. Not only have our practices and gathering rituals disappeared or changed, but the stories we share and the ways we explain or try to make meaning of our current situation also differ. The management of COVID-19 in the United States largely has unfolded on a local and individual level. We have few shared narratives of the coronavirus experience to hold us together.

For some, a sense of basic human decency has been lost with new revelations about the terrible things people are capable of. Others have had their fears confirmed. We have been bombarded by disturbing images: customers screaming at a Walmart greeter asking them to put on a mask, police bursting into Breonna Taylor's apartment, mass groups of partiers gathering despite CDC warnings, Derek Chauvin with his knee on the neck of George Floyd, violent insurrectionists storming the US Capitol. Amidst these cascading crises, some of our own neighbors have refused to wear masks or accept vaccines, despite numerous studies and threat of legal action. How we make sense of these events—the stories we tell ourselves and each other—affect community cohesion and trust moving forward.

Maintaining any relationship safely in a pandemic may necessitate high trust. Yet experiences of collective trauma dismantle trust in our various circles of community. Experiences of distrust can extend all the way from losing confidence in oneself to distrust in intimate relationships and families; in community networks and institutions such as schools, employers, and church; and in broader systems of government and even forces of nature.[17] Indeed, amid the traumatic impact of pandemic, racism, and social unrest, many also experienced the effects of climate change through horrific wildfires, floods, and multiple hurricanes. At the time of this writing, surviving citizens of Mayfield, Kentucky, are sifting through the debris of their homes and lives after a massive tornado nearly three-fourths of a mile in diameter swept through in a staggering 220-mile touchdown.

Even in the best situations, stress can instigate relational challenges such as rigidity, impatience, black and white thinking marked by an inability to see multiple points of view, and blaming. Many are experiencing burnout or compassion fatigue.

As with changes in self-identity, some positive relational changes may flourish after collective trauma. Healing and post-traumatic growth can lead to reconciliation between groups, a greater sense of intimacy or connection within a group, more freedom in being fully honest and open in relationships, and showing compassion toward the suffering of others.[18]

The word *compassion* means to "suffer with," but it is also often associated with a sense of agency around helping or alleviating suffering. Compassion is an attribute of God, moving God to act on behalf of those who are oppressed and suffering (see Psalm 86:15).

Tellingly, one of the Hebrew words translated as *compassion* in scripture is also related to the word for *womb*.[19] While compassion may feel like a finite resource for us, God's compassion is fecund, abundant, generative, and moves towards creation. Jesus' healing ministry was marked by fruitful compassion, extending self towards others. The Holy Spirit comes to us as a comforter and advocate in painful moments so that we are never without the presence of God. The work of the Spirit in us can help us grow in compassion towards others, and sharing stories of compassion can help to stitch together the frayed edges of community.

Trauma changes our stories about the past and future

Traumatic experiences can adversely affect worldview and the ability to plan for or imagine a future. Unprocessed trauma steals energy and can trap survivors from moving forward. When any members of a community are suffering in this way, the collective ability to process and plan is harmed. People and communities tend to plan and dream of the future in story form, but the unpredictable nature of the pandemic has made planning a challenge in all facets of life. Trauma may unravel faith or cause intense anger towards God for causing hopes and plans to unravel as well. There may be a general belief that life in our world unfolds with a kind of cruel capriciousness lurking everywhere, a sense of "waiting for the other shoe to drop."

For some, the storming of the US Capitol building on January 6, 2021, was traumatic. Four police officers who responded to the riot later committed suicide. Many of my friends, people who only experienced this event from a distance through the lens of news coverage, had their worldview around power transitions deeply shaken. Some expressed strong disbelief that the upcoming presidential power transition might unfold peacefully or without incident. Such deep fear, hopelessness, and fatalism is constraining and soul-numbing.

When the worst happens, it becomes integrated into the story of the future, polluting a sense of possibility, change, or redemption. "Grievance stories" are created when we rehearse a painful event over and over, using the same account until it becomes part of us and our way of being in the world.[20] Creating a grievance story may be a way to exercise agency in situations where people feel powerless, but part of the nature of a grievance story is that we can often be unaware of how its power operates in the background of our lives.

Grievance stories become stronger when we highlight a pattern of negative experiences and make these an implicit part of our identity. For example, leadership transitions happen in every congregation. Sometimes these transitions are traumatic, as in the case of a sudden death of a pastor or a pastor being removed for illegal or inappropriate behavior. A common grievance story I have encountered at several churches is "Pastors always leave our church." Every time a pastor leaves, the congregation reinforces this story.[21] Unresolved emotions from previous leadership transitions may emerge, and rituals associated with the transition may cause some to experience stress responses related to cumulative experiences of abandonment. Over time, grievance stories can become like an application running in the background of our lives that drains battery strength and slows everything down.

Many communities have grievance stories that shape behaviors. Some of the grievance stories that have shaped congregations and institutions where I have served include "Pastors never stay at our church"; "We don't have enough resources"; "The denomination wants to shut us down"; "We are a dying church"; and "We can't trust our leaders." Each of these phrases represents a painful narrative that has been reinforced over time and has contributed to collective identity and set of practices. When newcomers encounter these narratives, they may initially find them jarring. But if they stay, eventually they will be likely to come to accept these stories, at least implicitly.

One's sense of what is of ultimate significance can be rocked to the core by a traumatic event. Basics once assumed can suddenly become painfully precious. This sense of the unimportant falling away can also bring clarity of purpose and a sense of renewal to what remains.[22] Yet, even amid ongoing psychological discomfort caused by mass trauma, individuals and groups can also begin to explore how to live life in the fullest way possible, entering into the dynamics of limits and freedom to begin to exercise a sense of agency in how to move forward.

For people of faith, post-traumatic theological storytelling is part of processing traumatic experience and making meaning. It is completely normal and natural for traumatic experiences to cause congregations to question identity and mission in the face of trauma's ability to shatter basic trust and assumptions about who God is for us in the world.

Resmaa Menakem names "clean pain" as a means of "walking into the pain"—that is, processing and creating room for growth and the possibility of living rather than spending energy avoiding the very pain we carry in our individual and corporate bodies.[23] Theologically, Jesus models a way of clean pain by facing the powers that sought to kill him and end his healing ministry on the cross. Jesus' own path through this pain clears a space for us to also face our brokenness, sin, and finitude with courage and hope.

STORYTELLING AFTER TRAUMA

Storytelling has many individual collective benefits that can be especially helpful following traumatic events or stressful seasons:[24]

- Storytelling helps us to know and understand ourselves, each other, and God.
- Storytelling can build compassion.
- Hearing the stories of others can expand our perspective.
- Hearing stories can invite confession, repentance, and lament.
- Sharing stories can create a sense of unified purpose.
- Storytelling restores voices and perspectives that have been lost or silenced.
- Storytelling can establish a sense of identity, home, and belonging.
- Reconnecting with our most important stories can spark energy, rekindle vision, help guide next steps, and inspire future action.

- Storytelling reawakens memories and spurs us to praise God for past acts of saving, care, and provision.
- Stories are "free agents" and may surprise and challenge us.

The power of story

People are drawn to stories like moths to a flame. Kurt Vonnegut famously lectured on how stories were so basic and predictable that several simple forms could be plotted out on a graph. Vonnegut calls one of the most enticing forms "man in a hole."[25] "Man in a hole" doesn't technically need a man or a hole, but the basic plot unfolds like this: something or someone gets into trouble, they somehow get out of the predicament, and they end up better than they were before. This simple formulaic story appears in everything from books to films to commercials. Practically every detergent commercial ever made relies on this formula: child's baseball uniform gets dirty, specific brand of detergent is used; the clean uniform looks like new!

"Man in a hole" clearly has its place, but this formulaic story has also influenced the powerful self-help industry and even our understanding of the gospel itself.

Stories are so powerful; we need to treat them as a potent drug. They are how we relate our experiences. They shape our worldview. The intoxicating merger of the Christian story with what we most recently have called "prosperity gospel" but has also been called the "power of positive thinking" or even the more benign sounding "Protestant work ethic" is a toxic approach that puts us at a disadvantage when we experience trauma. Kate Bowler's memoirs bear witness to pain deepened by the discontinuity between this cultural narrative and her experience of cancer diagnosis, mortality, and finitude.

The world says, "You have power to shape your destiny. So if you experience pain, suffering, loss, misfortune, it's on you to fix it. Work harder! Be better! Say an empowering mantra daily and you will experience healing, success, a good life, etc." Traumatic experience completely undercuts this powerful narrative.

When a life-shaping narrative is unseated, we experience pain. When my sister-in-law Twila died suddenly of a brain aneurism in her thirties, she left behind very young children and close-knit work and church communities where she was loved and actively engaged. Her personality and life force were so large and her death so abrupt that I think our family will always live with a "Twila-shaped hole." One of the deepest narratives that was unseated for me amidst her traumatic loss was that of parents being able to raise their own children. Twila had plans short and long term for her family and her very young children. It seemed that these were lost when she died. As I parented a toddler and infant through my grief, a voice within me wondered, "What is the point of planning anything? How can I parent without any solidity of knowing that I will see this journey through?"

Sharing stories about Twila and her sudden loss, initially to family and close friends and eventually in writing, was vital to both making meaning amid the pain and moving forward.[26] Storytelling helps validate and remind our family of Twila's presence, dreams, faith, and the deep love that she had for her family. Twila's daughters were so young that they have no direct memories of their mother, but when I am with my young nieces today, I can experience the love that Twila poured into them. My hope is that the stories we share can also help them to know and understand a broader part of their identity as her daughters.

Not "any" story

My husband's family is only one generation removed from
the Amish. In the aftermath of Twila's death, our family was
sustained by the faith and love of a thick church community.
However, many today are not connected to communities that
can help sustain a sense of identity around shared story, shared
commitments, and shared practices. Without these vital tools,
our culture has nurtured consumerism as a primary means
of identity. This has implications not only for the practice of
lament (or lack thereof) but also our storytelling. While we
may sing, "They will know we are Christians by our love," we
are also very often known by the car we drive, the neighborhood we live in, or even the beverage we drink. At my local
Starbucks, I witnessed a woman brought to tears when her
usual drink wasn't made according to her stipulations. It can
be hard to withstand even tiny changes to the cultural nuances
that define us.

Christians speak of faith and identity in relationship to
Jesus' identity, actions, and behavior. As present-day disciples, we follow him, and we understand our suffering and
experiences of trauma and death through his experiences.[27]
Theologian Shelly Rambo writes, "The way of the cross, as
articulated throughout the tradition, shapes the Christian
imagination, providing a way for believers to map their relationship to suffering."[28]

Twentieth-century theologians have reckoned with the
symbolism of the cross in new ways, highlighting harmful
intersections between the Christian cross and the perpetration
of cultural trauma. Numerous theologians have contested
theological understandings that seem to lift up wounding,
suffering, and death in itself as redemptive. Christian participation in and the propagation of trauma and suffering arrests

our attempts at an easy or formulaic theology of the cross: the genocide of Jewish people, the lynching of African Americans, the coerced and conceptual "surrogacy" of Black women stripped of bodily agency, the dominance of patriarchal systems, the destruction of Indigenous lives and complete way of life at the hands of missionaries in residential schools.[29] These events, historical and ongoing, bear witness to the lasting nature of traumatic wounds.

Deconstructing our theology is necessary, but Jesus' complete identity, life, and experiences are part of God's redeeming love directed to us. At its best, a careful, nuanced, biblical, and humble theology of the cross and resurrection can help the church live in the wake of trauma.

Shelly Rambo's powerful and constructive exploration of the wounds on the resurrected Christ offers a hopeful path for survivors of trauma to theologically frame a sense of promise and new life that doesn't erase or deny traumatic experience but is "more than survival."[30] Trauma cannot be undone but it does not need to be the complete verdict on one's life. The wounds of the cross were present on the resurrected Christ, but they did not exercise control over him. The resurrection is a promise of *more*, of life beyond.

Early Christian gospel writers processed the earth-shattering experiences of the cross, resurrection, and aftermath in narrative form, but there is nothing theologically necessary about the *form* of a story. In his article on the limits of narrative, Richard Lischer writes, "Christianity generated stories that dramatize the untellable—the cataclysmic, the eschatological—in order to help others participate in the sign of Jonah and share in the fellowship of Christ's death and resurrection."[31] The gospel itself is much more complicated and much more valuable than a story (even "The Story") that defines us.[32] It is the life-changing power of God's direct engagement with humanity—most fully in the person of Jesus Christ—that has the power to sustain and help us regain a sense of identity, life, and possibility in the wake of trauma.

STORYTELLING AS A PRACTICE

Trauma disrupts our systems for making meaning in the world. The discontinuity between believing that bad things shouldn't happen to good people and the truth that no one gets a pass to excuse them from suffering and pain can throw us into disarray. Judith Herman notes that those who survive a traumatic experience may feel like they are losing their minds and that those who live with chronic traumatic stress may feel that they have completely "lost themselves."[33]

In a recent essay, David Brooks addresses "re-storying" after trauma. Re-storying involves sorting through fragmentation and brokenness to slowly create new narrative. He writes, "This process of post-traumatic growth is more like rewriting a novel than like solving a problem or healing a wound. It's a process of reconsidering and reorganizing—crafting a different story. This is one of those tasks, which most of us have to perform a few times over a life, that nobody teaches you about in school."[34]

In the immediate aftermath of trauma, storytelling may not be advisable. As noted earlier, only a trained mental health professional should attempt narrative therapy. When a person is not ready, sharing their story can grind in the pain and imprint harmful beliefs.[35] No one should be pressured to share their story. When people are ready, storytelling can be instinctual.

When the time for storytelling is appropriate, the ideas presented in the remainder of this chapter may help process trauma, strengthen and communicate identity and mission, and build a sense of connection among people.

Free writing

After my sister-in-law's sudden death, writing helped me to sort and reorganize internally. Writing has been a vital spiritual discipline that has fostered healing. Free writing can be practiced by individuals or groups. Free writing is when someone simply writes, without a prompt, without attending to grammar, spelling, or other mechanics of good writing. One can write whatever comes to mind for a set period. Even writing for fifteen to twenty minutes may help calm the nervous system and lower blood pressure.[36]

A writing group needs a set of practices that create space for safety, confidentiality, and courage as well as a balance of time for individual reflection and community connection. Circle processes using a talking piece slow communication down and make sharing more deliberate. Going around the circle allows everyone to have a turn or to pass if they do not wish to share. A friend facilitates writing circles at a local congregation. Rituals help to open and close the circle. Participants commit to the duration of the circle's existence, a set time, such as six to eight weeks. My friend has found that charging a small (sliding scale) fee helps with accountability.

Preaching

Stories are vital for preaching. Preachers can harness elements of good storytelling to help stories be effective tools for processing trauma. As Vonnegut pointed out, good stories have relatively standard ingredients and tools. We may have been taught in school that a story has a beginning, middle, and end. Good stories also tend to use senses to "show" rather than "tell." Stories that get us into the heart of the action tend to feel more exciting than stories with lots of set-up and description. Stories are like other art forms in that they work best when they allow the reader or listener to do some of the work, rather than telling us what the story meant.

Sermons can uproot grievance stories

Individuals and communities sometimes create grievance stories following traumatic experiences, which can fuel negative behaviors directed inward toward ourselves and outward toward others. Releasing a grievance story may involve raising awareness of the story and deliberate processing. This may include practices of lament and imagining the possibility of forgiveness.[37]

Stories always have a point of view, although the storyteller may not always be self-aware. Dr. Fred Luskin, who co-founded and directed the Stanford University Forgiveness Project, names a means of uprooting the destructive power of grievance stories: embracing varied points of view and analyzing the roles we play in the stories we tell. Instinctually, the stories we tell are from our own perspective and we may tend to cast people in our stories in stereotyped roles.[38]

"Black and white" stereotyped casting is a common trauma response. Following the 9/11 attacks, President Bush repeated referred to those involved in the attacks as "evildoers." Eventually, entire nations were classified as belonging to an "axis of evil."

While preachers should be consistent with point of view in a particular section of a sermon, varying perspective can be an effective means of highlighting implicit grievance stories and helping a congregation process. Quaker peace activist Gene Knudsen Hoffman notes, "An enemy is one whose story we have not heard."[39] I started seminary days after 9/11. Most of my professors scrambled to adapt syllabi to include units on Islam as a means of countering much of the negative backlash present in broader culture. In retrospect, I deeply appreciate this caring approach to expanding perspective in the wake of trauma.

At times, preachers may want to use stories of those who come from different backgrounds than the majority of our congregation to expand perspectives, uproot stereotypes and grievance stories, and humanize others. Telling the stories of people who live around the world can expand our sense of the arena of God's action. However, in this polarized and politically fragmented time, stories that do not resonate with listeners can run the risk of alienating or deepening a sense of disconnection to the church. Tracking the stories used in sermons over time is an important discipline for a preacher in order to balance perspectives.

Recognizing that every story has more than one point of view can help us realize when we may be digging into a harmful pattern. For example, a church that experiences a break-in may feel violated, betrayed, and targeted. This may play into a narrative of the congregation as a victim to forces outside its control. From another perspective, however, if many homes and businesses also experienced break-ins, the church may feel less targeted. If the church can hear a story of some who broke into a home or business in a moment of desperation, it may further destabilize a grievance story of victimhood.

Sermons can use story to build connection

Telling stories that disrupt stereotypes or pervasive cultural narratives can build human connection. Eight years ago, my friend John had the chance to visit Angola Prison in Louisiana with a dozen students. Angola is the largest maximum-security prison in the United States. Subsequently he has worked with students, inmate pastors, and others in several prisons and prison contexts. Those of us on the "outside" tend to define incarcerated people in terms of the worst thing that they ever did, the thing that landed them in prison. Those visiting prisons tend to see themselves as called to help "poor incarcerated people." Visitors are frequently surprised to find God among the incarcerated and themselves as beneficiaries of God's presence there.

As a preacher and seminary professor, John bears witness to God's transforming presence in prison through stories in his sermons, such as the story of Miguel Velez, who became an icon writer while serving a life sentence for murder in Angola Prison.[40] Focusing on transformation and beauty in a context of prison can help listeners understand that God's presence can touch difficult circumstances with healing, grace, beauty, and hope even as we are still grappling with difficult consequences of our own actions.

Sermons can use story as a rehearsal

Stories can also become a constructive "laboratory" where listeners can rehearse faithful action. In her book *Sunday's Sermon for Monday's World*, Sally Brown likens faithful Christian witness as bearing some similarity to jazz improvisation, as believers seek to live faithfully in-tune with the mercy, love, justice, and peace of God. Faithful discipleship, like jazz, is a richly storied experience with history, norms, skills, practices, and so on. Good jazz musicians and faithful followers of Jesus are able to engage with that deep formation in new ways that respond to the needs of particular times and places.[41]

Preaching that addresses the realities and needs of a local and particular congregation draws on deep formation alongside new and present realities. Brown encourages preachers to include stories of everyday Christian lives in preaching.[42]

This could also be done by inviting church members to share a word of witness as part of the sermon or in another part of the worship service. Participants can be encouraged to think about their day-to-day lives in the "wild," rather than the confines of church. How do they witness to faith as a student, office worker, or library volunteer?

Hearing a variety of stories in preaching, and from others, will help congregants deepen their repertoire of resources to draw upon for how to live faithfully. This is especially important during and following traumatic experiences, when usual patterns of behavior may have been disrupted and people need lifelines for how to live now.

My children are currently fans of the Harry Potter series. While I have my own literary critique and discomfort with her politics, author J. K. Rowling has done a phenomenal job of creating a world that captivates readers. Locations such as the Leaky Cauldron Pub, Diagon Alley, and Hagrid's Cottage are so vivid that my children imagine themselves into the story. Rowling's world has spawned a whole industry of products, sequels, films, and a theme park to feed the imaginations of readers.

While avoiding commodification, good preaching also invites listeners into other worlds—the worlds of the Bible and worlds represented by human experiences, troubled and touched by God here and now. Preachers want listeners to identify with the figures in our sermons, but perhaps more important is to help listeners explore stories to make connections and activate their own imaginations as a spiritual practice that helps them encounter the presence of the living God, inspiring and strengthening their broader witness in the world. Brown suggests one important tool for preachers is to resist telling the listeners what to think or the right way to interpret a story. Rather, preachers can follow the example of

Jesus' parables and let the story stand so it can function as a pathway to deeper reflection and growth within the community of listeners.[43] Empowering agency is also a powerful tool for helping survivors process and move forward following trauma.

Biblical storytelling: Knowing scripture by heart

Biblical storytelling is the practice of studying and internalizing the story of a passage of scripture before embodying it, with the goal of communication and bringing fuller meaning. The goal is not perfectly parroting a memorized text but incarnating it, with content accuracy over 90 percent and verbal accuracy over 70 percent. The biblical storyteller learns the story in a deep way rather than short-term memorization.

The first time I encountered biblical storytelling in worship, I was blown away. Rather than standing behind a lectern with little eye contact, the reader had learned the passage by heart. The young man stood in front of the lectern and moved as he recounted Jesus meeting the Samaritan woman at a well in John 4:4–26. His facial expressions, pauses, varied tempo, emphases, and inflection brought the story to life. Many years later, I helped a group at the seminary where I teach to tell this same biblical story as part of an interactive chapel service.

Tom Boomershine founded the Network of Biblical Storytellers in the 1970s, and it has been a powerful force for bringing scripture vividly to life in many congregations. Several years ago, Tom served as guest presenter in one of my worship classes. As part of his teaching about the practice, he shared a personal story that helped to catalyze storytelling as a means of embodied biblical interpretation. When Tom had just finished graduate school, he was struck by a car in a very serious accident.[44] Initially there was a concern that he would never walk again. He was in casts for six months and unable to walk without a cane for over a year. Other injuries in the accident made reading difficult. He drew deeply from the wells of his internal memory of scripture that he knew by heart. This deep encounter through internalized scripture nurtured him and gave him hope amidst agonizing and painful rehabilitation.

Tom's accident was physically catastrophic, but he also sustained damage to his sense of self and well-being. He struggled with guilt about not being able to run around and play with his young children because of the severity of his injuries. He experienced anger at God and malaise with the relentlessness of his physical therapy exercises and painful and slow progress. He was often doubtful as to whether he would walk and whether God could bring healing.[45] He struggled to maintain a sense of hope and perseverance with the difficult journey he was facing.

As Tom engaged in intense physical therapy and rehabilitation, the story of Jesus healing a paralyzed man in Mark 2:1–13 became *his* story as he internalized it in a deep way. Through this close encounter with scripture Tom experienced an important step of healing from the trauma of the accident. He writes:

> I began telling it to myself during the physical therapy in the hospital when I took my first steps between parallel bars: two steps the first day, four the next. But the most frequent tellings were during the months of physical therapy at home. When a knee is immobilized for a long period of time, adhesions grow over the joint. In order to get flexibility back, those adhesions must be broken. The easiest way is to push the joint as hard as you can, gradually breaking them. My task then was to sit and push as hard as I could as long as I could on that joint. After I couldn't stand the pain anymore, I could rest for a few hours before doing the same process again. This went on for months with only small

signs of progress. I told myself this story time after time during this period. . . . Day after day in a variety of ways, I told myself this story and remembered it in exquisite detail. Writing in my journal, prayer, and doing my exercises all became occasions for remembering this story. And in an equally varied number of ways, this story enabled me to recognize and accept Jesus' presence and power.[46]

Biblical storytelling may provide a means for congregations to process trauma collectively and for members to process individually. Congregations can choose a focal passage and work to learn it by heart. Different members can perform the text in worship and other congregational settings. Learning the text can be intergenerational and done in households, Sunday school classes, and small groups. Individuals may be supported by starting a biblical storytelling group that can meet as a Sunday school class or small group. There are many resources on the Network of Biblical Storytellers website, including print resources and videos to help leaders get started.[47]

Sharing our own stories

In the Disney movie *Inside Out*, we get a window into the internal life of a preteen girl, Riley. Riley's memories and self-identity are largely dominated by her personified inner figure of the emotion "Joy." Riley experiences intense stress through a cross-country move, a new school, the loss of key friendships, relational tension at home, and the many shifts that happen for kids as they enter adolescence. Her inner narrative and key memories shift to accommodate her new reality—this is a difficult and painful process but the sorting of memories, identifying experiences, and her changed sense of self lead to greater integration, growth, and the ability to hold sadness along with joy.

Congregations and groups may benefit from a corporate "inside out" experience. About six months into the COVID pandemic, the pastor of a local congregation interviewed its resident centenarian. At over the age of 102, she had survived the 1918 influenza pandemic as an infant and numerous other tragedies that unfolded over the past century. Her sharing was reassuring. I remember most her desire to return to "her place in the pew." Her "place" in the physical building was an important part of her sweeping life story.

Congregations house a wealth of stories. Members' own life stories, their own journeys of faith, intertwine with the past and present journey of the church. Like the Riley in *Inside Out*, some stories may have been shelved because they didn't match the prevailing identity of the church. Congregations may benefit from retrieving these stories and their wisdom. Conducting and recording interviews can be a wonderful way to tap into these stories and powerful memories. These stories also serve as reminders of God's presence and provision and our deepest identity and sense of calling as beloved children of God and witness to God's intentions for our world.

Interviews can easily be done over Zoom, recorded, and shared during worship or other congregational settings.[48] A pastor might interview a member, or it may nurture new connections to have a child interview a parent or an elder member in the congregation, or an elder member interview a child. Give a little coaching in advance about what makes for an open-ended question that will open up space for stories.

Another approach to tapping into a congregation's own story is represented in the congregational curriculum *Story Matters*. This resource guides a congregation through the process of exploring its past and present, creating a congregational timeline together and ultimately finding a biblical story that helps them understand their identity and purpose. The use of story rather than a mission statement is beneficial in that it is living and polyvalent. It links the present congregation with God's people through scripture and undergirds the Bible as foundation for the continuing identity of the congregation.

Timeline creation can be done in small groups or with a representative group of leaders or volunteers. The timeline of the church would include events occurring in the community (such as the building of a new school or the closing of a factory) or larger contexts (such as the September 11 attacks), key events in the life of the church (such as new pastor), and personal events (such as a wedding or baptisms.) After an initial "brain dump," events may be recorded on color-coded sticky notes, for example green for new ventures at a church or bold steps such as a building project, or pink for a crisis. [49] It may be helpful to note when many people name the same event and to see how personal, collective, and broader community events interact with each other.

Following the collaborative timeline creation, the curriculum guides a congregation in exploratory questions:

- "What opportunities and challenges are emerging from these stories?"
- "What themes are emerging about who we are as a congregation?"
- "What keeps coming up as an important aspect of who we have been or want to become?"[50]

Discernment leads to seeking a scriptural story that resonates with the life of the congregation. While churches can find their own, the curriculum also provides a list of examples. For example, Psalm 23 might go along with a sense of God's shepherding presence in good and hard times.[51] Picking one story may unfold as a winnowing process, and some congregations may end up with two stories.

Once a story is selected, congregations explore additional questions:

- "How does our story help us to hear God's call to us as individuals and as a congregation?"
- "How does our story help us to deepen the practices of our faith?"
- "What is God calling us to do through our story in our community and world?"[52]

Six-word memoirs

Six-word memoirs have found varying applications over the years.[53] The approach is straightforward. Leaders invite others to put together just six words to summarize their perspective on something or a season of life. Leaders can place a qualifier, such as six-word pandemic memoir or six-word memoir of faith. I have used it in my classes to get to know each other at the beginning of the term and with colleagues to reconnect. I have also used it with panelists at a conference to help them introduce themselves to the larger group. I can envision this tool being useful for a Zoom break-out time of brief sharing, or in small groups at a retreat, or as a regular practice for a youth group.

This short form of writing can unlock powerful sharing. In a clergy group, one participant shared his pandemic memoir, "My grandpa died. I miss him." For a panel discussion at a conference, one panelist's six-word memoir opened up a line of questions from the broader group about the balance of one's own faith challenges and experiences as a leader and how one seeks to encourage others. Appropriate and bounded vulnerability can open a space for others to be vulnerable too.

Magic box

On a visit to his childhood home shortly after we were married, my husband was sorting through things in a closet in an upstairs bedroom. Sorting through items inspired stories. A snow globe invoked memories of a trip in high school, a cowboy hat reminded him of when his sister went to a Garth Brooks concert. We found some older clothes that were so old they looked stylish again: a short shift dress made from an intricate metallic brocade and an ivory men's dress shirt with an interesting, embossed diamond pattern. We changed into the clothes and headed downstairs to surprise my mother-in-law. The shift dress had been her "going away dress" worn after her wedding. She made it herself from fabric that her new brother and sister-in-law had brought from India where they were serving as missionaries. The ivory shirt had been my father-in-law's "going away" shirt. My husband permanently "borrowed" his dad's shirt, which still hangs in our closet— and conjures up memories of that afternoon of storytelling whenever I come across it.

We are embodied and the things we save often have stories behind them. Churches are often home to closets and storage bins full of stories that help to shape our collective identity. To unlock these stories leaders can collect in a box items that are important for the church community. The best items are ones that will jog memories and elicit stories from those who are still in the congregation—make sure to use a mix of older and newer objects, for example, an old hymnal, or a sign and part of a costume from a recent vacation Bible school. The "magic memories box" could be used at a retreat or as part of worship for children's time.[54] Invite people to share the story or memory that is connected to each item. This can be adapted for in-person or online sessions.

*   *   *

This chapter has only scraped the surface of the potent power of storytelling and its deep connection to identity, priorities, mission, and behaviors. When trauma has rattled the core of a community, storytelling can re-center and ground us again. The witness of biblical parables reminds us that there are many paths of interpretation and that listeners participate in meaning-making. The exercise of agency with individuals and the larger group making meaning through story can allow for people with a wide range of perceptions and experiences to find a place. Congregations need to take care with story because our culture has generated a deep longing for stories of success, rags to riches, stories where we are the hero and always win. There is no space for the integration of traumatic experience or complex grief in these simplistic stories, and the lack of a coherent recognizable positive narrative can create another layer of loss. It is normal to struggle with lack of closure and coherence in this season of prolonged collective trauma around COVID-19.

The gospel story and the journey of the cross provide a vital counterbalance and important check for the stories we tell as Christians. However, our experience of good news and the presence of God is not reducible to story. The gospel is vast and sacred, and lives both within and beyond the limits of language.

FOUR

Blessing

Some words hold a potent power that exceeds the one who speaks. We think of Jesus' preaching as God's realm bursting into our world. Reading scripture and preaching today echoes this potent word-act. We can understand blessing in a similar way. Blessings are a manifestation or experience of God's love and goodness. Blessing is an overflow of God's very being that pours out on creation both indiscriminately and with specific intention. Blessings unfold in a particular place and time; what is construed as blessing is deeply contextual. Spoken blessings bear witness to God's presence in our world. When we bless, we name the world as already redeemed— we name the reality God intends for the world. Blessings can also invite God's presence into a situation or call upon people to exercise God-given agency in a situation. Blessings can be especially effective during transitions. A blessing offered as gathered worship concludes helps worshipers transition to day-to-day life and mission in our world.

Blessings are divine in origin but may be facilitated and perpetuated by people. To be blessed or called often comes with an imperative to share that blessing, to bear witness to God and God's vision for creation. God's covenant with Israel is steeped with a sense of giving and receiving blessing. In Genesis 12 God promises, "I will make of you a great nation, and I will bless you, and make your name great, so that you will be a blessing. I will bless those who bless you, and the one who curses you I will curse; and in you all the families of the earth shall be blessed." (Gen 12:2-3) Scripture confounds in that it often seems that those who have a special calling experience a significant amount of suffering in their journey. One thinks of favored son Joseph in Genesis 37–50 with his special coat, who is hated by his brothers, sold into slavery, and sent to prison before rising to a prominent role that saves his family and the future of Israel from starvation.

God relates to creation with specificity and intention. God chooses. The experience and actions of blessing are part of those experiences of choosing and being chosen. We rest in the grace that God ultimately chooses life, love, justice, mercy, and peace. God chooses to dwell with us and wipe away tears. In the meantime, we struggle with experiences of suffering and trauma in our world. We struggle because often we have no good choices or no choices at all. We must grapple with the hard questions. What does it mean to be singled out, "blessed," or "called"? What does it mean to not be the one who is chosen? How do we live when forces outside our control mean that we have no choices?

I am reminded of a haunting photograph from a student journalist's photo-essay. The essay explores the life of Keyla "Nunny" Reece during her treatment of stage four metastatic breast cancer. It features a picture of Nunny sleeping with the caption that this was when Nunny started home hospice care.[1] Nunny wanted the photos to help her young son understand her cancer journey. In the photo, we see a young woman sleeping in a hospital bed in her living room. Her head is bald, her forehead is furrowed, her face thinner than the earlier photos in the essay. The most arresting element of the image is a large white decorative throw pillow at the foot of the hospital bed with the word *blessed* in sparkling gold cursive script. The word *blessed* feels so incongruous with the image of the young mother's suffering, a cruel label that one cannot reconcile.

To be blessed is a gift and experience of grace. About eight years ago I was anxious and sad, about to announce that I would be resigning my position and moving to another seminary. Transitions are hard in part because they involve loss and rupture—even chosen transitions as this was, and happy transitions as this mostly was. I had already encountered one co-worker's response of hurt and blame around my decision to move. But my anxiety and sadness were diffused almost instantly by the gracious gift of another colleague's response. She turned to me, her eyes searching mine as she said, "I'm sad but I want to bless you." I have carried her blessing with me ever since. Just as we carry the scars and wounds from traumatic and stressful experiences in our individual and collective bodies, so too we can carry the marks of blessing.

Obviously, amid a global pandemic, "blessing" is a freighted topic. Often equated with material well-being that serves as "proof" of divine favor, or as a word used to close emails (guilty!) or when someone sneezes, the concept of blessing is rich biblically and theologically. This practice has great potential for communities in the aftermath of trauma. However, we need to clear the screen and reclaim it as a specifically Christian practice with more thoughtful theological anchors.

Our theology of blessing must incorporate the work and person of Jesus Christ. Jesus holds together the experiences of being deeply blessed by God but also taking on intense suffering. In Jesus, death is not a barrier to God's blessings.

Biblical scholar Claus Westermann writes that at times, "blessing shares in the hidden nature of God's work in the cross of Christ."[2] We cannot objectively measure or quantify blessing. It is marked by a sense of mystery.

Irish teacher and poet John O'Donohue writes, "It would be infinitely lonely to live in a world without blessing." O'Donohue writes from a Celtic spiritual tradition of blessing as illumined by a divine internal spark, a means of connection to "a harvest of memory, spirit, and dream that has long preceded us." For O'Donohue, the material world itself is a gift, our "first blessing."[3] When we offer blessings in the name of Jesus Christ and make the sign of the cross on someone's hand or forehead, we accept and affirm that God's work of blessing may be hidden in the cross, much as seeds are hidden deep in soil.[4] We can trust there is generative life present, though it may be hidden.

The previous two chapters explored the practices of lament and storytelling as tools for processing trauma. These practices reflect more obvious links to well-established therapeutic tools. Blessing feels different because it is not commonly placed in conversation with trauma. Including blessing in the conversation changes it and provides an unexpected, additional tool for nurturing resilience in people of faith. Part of the power of blessing lies in the confounding theological tension at its heart. We tend to view blessing as evidence of God's presence in the form of material well-being or as a means of preemptively warding off harm, yet in Jesus Christ we also experience God's blessing hidden in the cross.

This chapter provides a brief overview of blessing from a biblical and theological perspective with an eye for equipping pastors and leaders to thoughtfully engage in this practice. Before embracing the gifts of the practice, it is also important to name some of the cultural hurdles and challenges related to blessing as a practice for the church. As with previous chapters, my aim is practical, offering ways that individuals and groups can use the practice of blessing to process traumatic stress and move toward a sense of healing.

BLESSING IN THE BIBLE

In the Old Testament, God's agency is oriented towards saving and accompanying God's people. Deliverance and blessing are two related actions.[5] Deliverance involves God's intervention to save, and blessing serves as a sign and signal of God's continued presence and care.[6] Blessing is not salvific, but it is oriented around comfort, security, safety, health, and good fortune.[7] Claus Westermann argues that separating the "delivering" and "blessing" acts of God leads to a sense of reduction, a focus on a moment of salvation rather than a full sense of life lived with God.[8] The celebration of sacraments serve as a powerful means of holding together a fuller sense of the actions of God.

Blessings start with God but can be passed from person to person. Biblical blessings largely involve divine provision, fertility, prevailing against one's enemies and possession of wisdom.[9] God's promise to Abraham in Genesis 12 is emblematic: "I will make of you a great nation, and I will bless you, and make your name great, so that you will be a blessing. I will bless those who bless you, and the one who curses you I will curse; and in you all the families of the earth shall be blessed" (vv. 2–3). Blessings are passed from one family member to another and from priest to the people.[10] Isaiah's messianic prophecy speaks of a sense of blessing as connected to wisdom. The prophet writes, "The spirit of the LORD shall rest on him, the spirit of wisdom and understanding, the spirit of

counsel and might, the spirit of knowledge and the fear of the
LORD" (Isaiah 11:2).

In the New Testament, blessings are offered in continu-
ity with Old Testament practices. The Christ event and the
presence of Christ are integrated into this rich tradition.[11] For
example, at the end of Luke's gospel, Jesus explicitly blesses
the disciples as he ascends to heaven (see Luke 24:50–53). The
gift of the Holy Spirit is part of this blessing, which the disciples are called to extend. Jesus' followers continue in a state of
blessedness and blessing.

The celebration of communion instituted in the New
Testament is a potent form of blessing.[12] In what we know
as the Last Supper, Jesus blessed the bread before breaking
it and sharing it with his disciples. This was no longer ordinary bread; in the hands of Jesus it had become his own body
(Matthew 26:26; Mark 14:22). Blessed, broken, shared. When
sacramental traditions celebrate communion, the Spirit of
God is poured out on the elements and participants. Both are
blessed in a potent and generative way that enlivens faith and
empowers the Christian life.

It is the Christ event that offers us a way to live in the
presence of the tension of blessing in the aftermath of trauma.
Jesus and his closest companions experience profound blessing, which does not guard them from the experiences of suffering and trauma. Mary's pregnancy with Jesus is a blessing,
to which Elizabeth bears witness in Luke: "Blessed are you
among women, and blessed is the fruit of your womb" (Luke
1:42). And yet, as Simeon's blessing poignantly prophesied,
"a sword will pierce [Mary's] soul" (Luke 2:34–35). She will
certainly suffer trauma as her son's earthly ministry ends in
a horrific public execution on a Roman cross. Jesus' life also
seems absent the signs of blessing we might expect. He was

hated, despised, and betrayed by his own people, including his closest friends. He was tortured and killed by a powerful political empire. This is not the picture of a "#blessed" life of ease, warmth, health, and wealth. But it does bear some resemblance to the picture of Nunny, suffering on her hospital bed, living her final days with dignity, intention, and love. Broken and blessed.

One could write many books on the topic of biblical blessings. While my comments here are not comprehensive, the points that follow offer some structure for leaders and congregations to think about blessing as a practice and to begin to unpack the complex dynamics around blessing. To start, here are some themes related to blessing that we find across scripture and theology. These could be used when teaching or preaching about blessing.

Blessing bears witness

Bearing witness is an important aspect of attending to trauma in our world. Turning away from situations of pain can be instinctual. We may deny or dissociate from our own painful wounds and the wounds of others. The Holy Spirit can help us choose truth, solidarity, and accompaniment. Witnesses can validate and normalize traumatic responses and offer support to survivors.

Because the power of blessing lies with God rather than with those who speak the words, spoken blessings can be understood as acts of witness that point to the reality of God's blessings that may extend beyond the present moment. This understanding is similar to the celebration of the Lord's Supper or baptism for those in church traditions that celebrate signs and ordinances and trace their roots to Ulrich Zwingli. These sacred actions point to God's prior and ongoing action.

Blessing can bear witness to God's healing intentions for everyone—even when those are still unfolding in situations of brokenness and pain. Survivors may bear witness to healing and wholeness even as it is still unfinished.

Psalm 103's exuberant testimony uses the language of blessing as a form of witness. The shadow of pain and brokenness stand in the background, and the psalmist blesses the Lord for saving acts.

> Bless the LORD, O my soul,
>   and do not forget all his benefits—
> who forgives all your iniquity,
>   who heals all your diseases,
> who redeems your life from the Pit,
>   who crowns you with steadfast love and mercy,
> who satisfies you with good as long as you live
>   so that your youth is renewed like the eagle's.
> (Psalm 103:2–5)

The psalmist continues, reflecting key touchstones of God's saving faithfulness and love extended toward Moses and Israel, focusing on mercy and compassion, God's power, and human finitude. Such reflection inspires the blessing. To reflect on God almost compels praise and blessing from the psalmist's lips.

Blessing restores relationships

Reconnecting to community is an essential aspect of processing traumatic experience.[13] Strong relationships can also nurture resilience. Some years ago, a woman in one of my classes shared a ritual from her family that instilled resilience. Each day before her children went to school, she would lay a hand on each child's head and repeat the Aaronic blessing from the book of Numbers:

> The LORD bless you and keep you;
> the LORD make his face to shine upon you, and be gracious
> to you;
> the LORD lift up his countenance upon you, and give
> you peace.
> (Numbers 6:24–26)

This ritual became an enduring part of Christian formation in their family and a way of showing love and care that sustained them in difficult times. She continued to offer this blessing as her children aged through school, and it was especially powerful to lay a hand of blessing on her sons, now taller than her, before leaving them in their dorms at college.

Preaching on the same blessing from Numbers, pastor Brian Maguire used historical research to portray a scene of trauma in the life of Israel in which this blessing served as an agent of God's care and love within a family.

> What do you do when your world appears to be crashing down around you? Do you panic? Do you flee? Do you hide? That was the question that faced Yohannan ben Moshe during the long hot summer of 585 BCE, or at least that is how I imagine it. His world was coming to an end, and he knew it. With each passing month more refugees came pouring into Jerusalem from northern villages overrun by Babylonian armies. He had trouble obtaining good quality wool for his looms. It did not really matter, because people were in no mood to buy his cloth. They were fixed on the growing menace just over their horizon. The hosts of Babylon were approaching like a cloud of locusts destroying everything in their path. Every night he squeezed Dinah, his little daughter, hoping to somehow fill her with enough love to sustain her through the storm he knew was coming. He overindulged her as best he could on a weaver's pay. He knew what was coming but could do nothing

to protect her from it. Some of the wealthy now moved away to escape. Others prayed for God to save them. Isaiah and Jeremiah kept ranting against King Jehoiakim and his schemes. But none of that really mattered to Yohannan. All that mattered to him was Dinah.

What do you do when your world appears to be crashing down around you? Yohannan had an idea. He gathered up his few spare shekels and went to the silversmiths in the southern part of the city. He asked them to make an amulet for his daughter. Something to keep her safe. Something to guide her through the dark days ahead. Something to remind her that no matter the circumstances of her life, she was loved. They knew what to do. They pounded the silver into a tiny little scroll. In careful letters they pressed the holy verse. They rolled it up in a tight cylinder and threaded a cord through it. Yohannan went home and slipped the tiny silver necklace around Dinah's neck, telling her to never take it off no matter what. He told her that it was his and God's blessing for her and for her life.

No one knows what happened next. Perhaps Dinah accidentally left the necklace behind. Perhaps she handed it down to her grandchildren, who dropped it years later. Perhaps she met her fate when the Babylonians destroyed the city the following summer. All we know is someone dropped the necklace in a shallow cave just west of the Old City of Jerusalem, where it sat for over twenty-five centuries until 1979 when a young archeologist cleaning up garbage in the cave picked it up and paused. It looked like a filthy cigarette butt, but it felt odd. She gave it to her supervisor Gabriel Barkay.

It took twenty years to figure out how to unroll it without breaking it. Finally, with exquisite care, archeologists unrolled the scroll, and the words that emerged from twenty-five centuries of silence were immediately familiar to everyone: "May the Lord bless you and keep you; may the Lord make his face to shine upon you, and be gracious to you; may the Lord lift up his countenance upon you, and give you peace." What they had found was not an old cigarette filter but the oldest known biblical text ever discovered. Perhaps even more important, they had found an artifact of one person's love and hope for another.[14]

In the Bible, blessings are deeply relational acts that involve divine agency. Blessings involve God even when blessing happens between people. As a child, I remember struggling (as I still struggle) to understand the account in Genesis 27 of the blessing from our ancestor in the faith, Isaac, that was intended for Esau and stolen by Jacob. The complex competitive relational dynamics between twins seem to pollute a holy sense of blessing.

In contrast to a generous expansive theological view of God's blessing demonstrated by my former student and pastor Maguire's sermon, with this story we may ask how human blessing can fall so short. How could a parent's blessing be so finite, limited and bound by material understandings of a scarce resource? I ache for Esau, the unblessed who cries for a blessing, "Have you only one blessing, father? Bless me, me also, father!" And Esau lifted up his voice and wept." (Genesis 27:38). I wonder how Isaac, Esau, Rachel, and Jacob could have such limited imagination.

Blessing serves a purpose

In the Bible, blessing isn't an empty act. It is done for a reason. For example, in the Old Testament, blessing is often a means of bearing witness to God's presence with our faith ancestors.[15] Blessings are given as a form of testimony to who God is in such a way that being in relationship with God is seen as attractive to others.[16]

Blessing is also a tool of maintaining covenant between God and people. God's promises extended to Abraham and his children are experienced as blessings, but Israel is not a passive recipient. Blessings are part of a well-maintained relationship where Israel needs to respond with righteous living and worship. Indeed, part of the relational response to blessings from God is to respond with praise.[17]

The book of Job is extremely complex, but we do see God using blessing as a tool to justify Job to his friends who refused to believe that he was indeed blameless for the suffering he experienced (Job 42).

Wisdom literature highlights connections between an individual's righteous living and the experience of blessing. It follows that one experiences withholding of blessing as a consequence of not living rightly. Right living encompasses fear of the Lord and following God's law, which has social dimensions as well. For example, Proverbs 3:33 summarizes much of the teaching for wise and prudent living outlined in the whole in terms of blessing and cursing, "The LORD's curse is on the house of the wicked, but he blesses the abode of the righteous."[18]

Blessing is not transactional

A simplistic transactional understanding of blessing denies the complexities of God and humanity. Virtuous human behaviors are not coins inserted into a divine vending machine that shoots out blessings. Scripture does not support a vending machine faith.

In the Sermon on the Mount, Jesus instructs his followers to do good to those who persecute them because God sends blessings (sunshine and rain) on those who are both just and unjust (Matthew 5:45). While God's blessings and power are not under our control, disciples of Jesus are called to extend God's love broadly even toward those who may have caused them harm.

One of the most challenging aspects of processing trauma is coming to terms when survivors see themselves as "having done everything right." I regularly encounter a tension in preaching linked to experiences of suffering and trauma. Those who have encountered intense suffering will often ascribe their experience to "God's will" because the alternative, that this horrible thing has happened randomly, is too terrible to bear. This theological approach holds that it is better to live in a world with a God who wills pain and suffering for a reason than to live in a world where God appears to be inactive or inscrutable.

The same theology holds true when good things happen. God is the power behind everything. I have noticed this theology most present among those who have experienced systemic social suffering, racism, and structural oppression.

A benefit of this approach is a frank openness in turning to God amid all circumstances, both terrible and joyful. God is viewed as active and engaged, working for our benefit, even in suffering. Those who hold to this theology trust that God has a greater good in mind. For those caught in unjust systems such as racism, this approach testifies to faith in a God who is ultimately in charge. There is a bigger picture yet to be revealed. This approach is very grounding for the practice of lament.

An alternative theological approach holds that God's ways are far beyond our understanding. God has given humans agency and the ability to make choices. The world is fallen. Sometimes terrible and wonderful things may seem from our perspective to "just happen." This view is also held by those who have experienced intense suffering, but the suffering is often less systemic and more personal. Sometimes, this theology takes a larger eschatological view like the approach just discussed, but is willing to consign some acts to mystery rather than attribute them directly to God. A benefit of this approach is that it avoids assigning terrible acts to the hand of God, which can alleviate some suffering among the faithful who struggle to understand what they did wrong or why God might do this to them.

Parsing omnipotence can feel like a fool's errand at worst and at best a theological pacifier to fill an aching void when the unthinkable has happened. God's actions in the person of Jesus show so poignantly that our understanding of power is often misguided. God does not do what we think God should do. In Jesus, God suffers and dies on a cross. In a recent issue of *Christian Century*, editor Peter Marty proposes that God's very being as "love" means that God limits God's power to truly be with us, loving us deeply in experiences of suffering and struggle in solidarity so thick that God becomes human, suffers and dies, and abides, advocates, and prays with us every moment as Holy Spirit.[19]

John O'Donohue reminds us that blessing is a direct and specific way of giving care within particular circumstances or contexts. Blessing is not generic. O'Donohue writes, "The blessing form has an eye to the outside in order to embrace and elevate whatever is happening to someone. It is direct address, driven by immediacy and care." Blessing intentionally honors human experience in its excruciating individuality.

Blessing is God's grace among us
In their theological simplicity and formative power, children's songs can be profound or painfully reductionistic. During the

pandemic, I listened from another room while my children sang about how "the wise man built his house upon the rock." Jesus' teaching at the end of the Sermon on the Mount uses the metaphor of building a house on a rock or on sand to bring home the importance of living according to Jesus' difficult ethic (Matthew 7:24–27). However, the children's song takes a turn that is not present in Matthew. Singers are instructed to "build their homes on the Lord Jesus Christ," and "blessings will come down." The final chorus risks a transactional understanding of blessing. "Oh, the blessings come down as your prayers go up."

Unlike in this children's song, blessings in scripture are prayers invoking the presence of God, offered with awareness of God's identity and freedom. As noted above, God's blessings are freely given gifts of grace, not transactions.

Serving communion and being served is an extremely powerful experience of blessing and grace. I remember a particularly downtrodden moment in graduate school. I was questioning my path and wondering if I would secure a job. During the campus chapel worship, a beloved mentor pressed an extra-large hunk of bread into my palm and said, "This is Christ's body for you, Joni." In an experience of grace, my spirit was revived. This is tangible, physical, blessing-in-action. The elements are blessed, and that blessing is extended through the community of faith as the Spirit of God freely pours out upon the elements and the people.

In my own Mennonite tradition, children who are not yet baptized do not typically receive communion. Some of my most cherished memories in ministry involve handing the bread to brothers and sisters in Christ and blessing children. When children come through the communion line, they might cross their arms over their chest to signal their desire for a blessing. To bless these beloved children of God is a powerful action that signifies a sense of belonging to God and God's realm. The experience of being blessed can be understood as a sign of God's realm among us.

Blessing as a practice can invoke and invite an experience of grace associated with God's reign. Using the word *may* in blessing "imagines and wills" divine presence to the particular pains and joys in our lives. Blessing shows us where God is present in our experience and encourages. O'Donohue's blessing *For Longing* leans into this sense of encouragement and invitation.

> May you have the courage to listen to the voice of desire
> That disturbs you when you have settled for something safe.[20]

Blessing is release

Blessing can also be a way of letting go and moving forward. In Genesis 32:22–32, our biblical ancestor in the faith, Jacob, is troubled on the eve of reuniting with his brother Esau. He sends his family and flocks ahead and remains at the ford of the Jabbok. He does not sleep and spends the night wrestling with a man/being of divine origin and strength. As the first rays of dawn scatter silvery light on the banks of the river, the struggle grows more desperate. Jacob will not submit, and in the heat of the fight, his divine opponent puts his hip out of joint. Even hobbled by injury, Jacob will not release the man unless he is blessed. When his demand is answered, Jacob lets go. He is blessed with a new name, and new possibilities for relating to others. When Jacob meets Esau later that day, the history of betrayal between them has been released. The brothers embrace and are each able to move forward. Jacob offers gifts to Esau not out of a sense of requirement but as an extension of God's blessing. He says to his brother, "To see your face is like seeing the face of God—since you have received me with such favor. Please accept my gift that is brought to you, because God has dealt graciously with me." Esau, no longer bound by a drive for vengeance, accepts Jacob's gift (Genesis 33:10–11).

When we struggle and are unable to let go of a conflict, regret, action, relationship, or other experiences of brokenness, blessing can be a tool of grace to release people or experiences into God's care and move forward.

Blessing in a disenchanted world

Understanding blessing in the ancient world is difficult for us in the present. The figures in the Bible lived in a world that was charged with divine presence and dripping with deeper significance. For biblical figures, invoking God's power in blessing and curse had real power in the lives of people and the physical world.

As philosopher Charles Taylor reminds us, our world today is "disenchanted."[21] We view ourselves as autonomous and in control of our lives. We focus on that which is immanent and measurable and have little sense of transcendence. This can make blessings feel akin to polite vaguely religious exchanges, like "please" and "thank you" for pious types.

For example, most of us approach depression as a mental illness, something chemically out of balance in the brain that can be helped by medication, rather than as demon possession. This would not have been the perspective of those in the ancient world. We can trace shifts in understanding transcendence and God's power through interpretations of passages such as the Gospels' portrayal of the intense suffering of a Gerasene man with an unclean spirit in Mark 5:1–20. When visiting the land of the Gerasenes, Jesus and his disciples encounter a man living among the tombs. He has been repeatedly chained and shackled in a place of isolation and death to keep him from causing harm to himself. The text tells us that he does not sleep but rather howls day and night and that despite repeated attempts to restrain him, he has bruised himself with stones. Clearly the man in the text is in deep torment. My preaching students tend to downplay demonic action and focus on the suffering man's isolation, marginalization, and social suffering. These harms at the hands of the man's community may be easier to understand than the man being possessed by a legion of evil spirits that Jesus casts into a herd of pigs.[22]

Nevertheless, the concept of blessing rests on an understanding that God directly engages with us—something that can feel like a stretch for some of us in late modernity. Yet even for those who are thoroughly secular, in times of uncertainty, anxiety, and transition, one may be open to experiencing something "other" beyond the here and now.

The Celtic spiritual sense of "thin places" may provide a set of lenses to help us understand experiences of God's blessing in our disenchanted world. Thin places are specific physical geographic locations, often linked to our natural world, where the boundary between the sacred and everything else is permeable, where one can feel the presence of God in a thick and visceral way. For example, George McCleod, who engineered the rebuilding of the abbey on the island of Iona, was motivated by experiences of the immediate presence of God and the "thinness of the line that divides this world and the next."[23] Iona continues to be a popular destination for spiritual pilgrimages.[24]

However, another point of view is that the experience of a "thin place" has much more to do with us and our own openness than with God's decision to be more present in some places than others. Speaker and author Eric Weiner proposes that travel to thin places "disorients and confuses."[25] After college I spent a summer working at a Christian summer camp. Children and teens regularly had powerful experiences of deepened faith. For some it was linked to the sense of the beautiful outdoors; for others it was the intense focus on Christian curriculum, time for prayer and spiritual practices each day, and the support of camp staff and cabin buddies. Camp was a thin place where many returned each summer. When people experience new spaces, a change of pace, and the absence of routines that put us in a state of living on autopilot, it is more likely that we will encounter a thin place.[26]

Places become "thin" to us when we are vulnerable and open to God, when we set aside our pretense of control.[27] The same may be true of God's blessings. Weiner writes, "If God (however defined) is everywhere and 'everywhen' as the Australian aboriginals put it so wonderfully, then why are some places thin and others not? Why isn't the whole world thin? Maybe it is because we're too thick to recognize it. Maybe thin places offer glimpses not of heaven but of earth as it really is, unencumbered. Unmasked."[28]

In the book *Getting to God*, Luke Powery, John Rottman, and I build a case that situations of deep trouble are often the spark for a thin place of divine encounter, of blessing. We hold that Christian proclamation can also be a thin place, particularly when it bears witness to experiences of God's action and presence in the Bible and in our world.[29]

While transcendence and the idea of thin places are difficult concepts even for believers to pin down as we live our mostly secular lives, we do regularly encounter moments where our experience is more—deeper, more charged than what we can explain with our natural senses. The sacraments, where bread and cup become the body and blood of Christ for us, and the saving significance of the waters of baptism are situations where the church regularly encounters thin places of transcendence, blessing, and grace. The practices of keeping sabbath and worship offer a change in day-to-day rhythms and a focus on God that can create a thin space. Within worship, the reading and proclamation of scripture may also open a thin place for worshipers, where the words we take in become more than words, a means to connect with God and faithful believers present and across time and space.

Our world is disenchanted, but Taylor also sees our world as "haunted" by transcendence. One may think about how many love the magical world of Harry Potter or our broader cultural fascination with zombies and vampires or with unexplained phenomena. In this vulnerable and traumatic pandemic season, many of us have engaged in a mix of solid science-backed behaviors such as mask-wearing and distancing as well as hope-filled "magical thinking" around COVID.

Magical thinking is an emotional crutch that allows us to get by, but it does not take the place of actual faith. Magical thinking was in full display early in the pandemic when the Trump administration expressed a desire/hope/intention that the pandemic might be over by Easter of 2020. As I write more than two full years later, the pandemic has ebbed and flowed and the world still faces serious threats from highly transmissible variants. My own family engaged in magical thinking while waiting for vaccine availability for our young children. We talked about all the things we could do when the kids were finally vaccinated. In truth, a vaccine is not a "get-out-of-pandemic-free" card. Post-vaccine activities still come with risk, and as parents we still have difficult decisions to make.

Magical thinking is different from a robust sense of divine power that is greater than human power or plans. My pastor friend Brian Maguire holds that many people feel a sense of spiritual lack but don't recognize the transcendence they are missing. In an email exchange he describes gently nudging his congregation into deeper spiritual waters "to tempt people with tastes of transcendence that may stimulate their desire for more. . . . The way famine relief workers place drops of sugar water on starving children's lips to trigger their hunger and digestive system to reactivate. For many we are so far from the transcendent that our first task seems to be to remind them what they are missing."[30]

BLESSING AS A PRACTICE
Scripture refers to two forms of the practice or experience of blessing.

1. Blessing can be a ritual with specific language offered by a priest or other representative mediating God's action or presence to individuals or groups in worship.
2. Blessing can be a free act of God who is not bound by form or setting.[31]

These two pathways echo a biblical understanding of worship that holds together God's freedom and God's promises to draw near us in specific times and places; the God who surprises Moses in a burning bush and the God who promises to bring God's glory to the Holy of Holies.

In worship today, practices of blessing can feel like an elastic category that may hold words, actions, and spiritual postures. The setting and experience of the group or congregation plays a significant role in how blessing as a practice may help with processing traumatic stress.

Writing a blessing

It is not necessary to write a new blessing for every situation, but it can be therapeutic for leaders or groups to create a blessing for a specific situation. Because God is relational rather than transactional, prayers should be rooted in who God is and who we are rather than being mostly a list of things that we want from God.

Blessings can be free in form, like poetry which finds its own rhythm. When a blessing is addressed actively to God, beginning, "May the God/Spirit/One who . . .," it acknowledges our relationship with God and helps keep the blessing from seeming like a transaction. Consider this example blessing from the hymnal *Voices Together*:

> May the Christ who walks
> on wounded feet
> walk with you on the road.
> May the Christ who serves
> with wounded hands
> stretch out your hands to serve.
> May the Christ who loves
> with a wounded heart
> open your heart to love.
> May you see the face of Christ
> in everyone you meet,
> and may everyone you meet
> see the face of Christ in you.[32]

Sometimes God's presence and power are implicit in a blessing that is created to acknowledge human experience and affirm and support human agency. While God is not named, human blessing flows from God. God's presence undergirds the address, "Blessed are they/is the one who . . . ." For example, Kate Bowler offers, "A Blessing for Keeping Your Heart Soft When Everything Is Broken":

> Blessed are you who see it all now. The terrible, beautiful truth that our world, our lives seem irreparably broken. And you can't unsee it. The hungry kid. The exhausted mom. The woman who wonders if any of this is worth it. The loneliness and despair.
>
> Blessed are you who glimpse reality and don't turn away. This kind of seeing comes at a steep cost, and it is a cost you may not have paid intentionally, but here you are. Seeing things clearly. Blessed are you who have worked hard to keep your heart soft. You who live with courage, fixing what is in your reach, praying about what is not, and loving, still.
>
> May you experience deeper capacity and glimpses of hope, as you continue to see the world as it is. Terrible. Beautiful.[33]

John O'Donohue writes this blessing, "For Someone Awakening to the Trauma of His or Her Past":

> . . . As your tears fall over that wounded place,
> May they wash away your hurt and free your heart.
> May your forgiveness still the hunger of the wound
>
> So that for the first time you can walk away from that place,
> Reunited with your banished heart, now healed, and freed,
> And feel the clear, free air bless your new face.[34]

Inviting God's blessing and God's intervention

Blessing engages both divine and human agency and bears some resemblance to practices of forgiveness or release. These can be deeply meaningful practices when the time is right and when a person or group is ready. These same practices can also deepen trauma or harm when forced upon one who has experienced pain, betrayal, and brokenness at the hands of others.

Blessing can be incorporated into a prayer that might be offered using the language of asking for God's blessing and God's intervention. We can pray that God might intervene in circumstances in our world that display signs of brokenness and violence. This prayer of release may open us up to hearing where the Spirit may be inviting us to intervene in God's name, or we may simply release these situations into God's care. We can ask God's blessing in situations in our world that show signs of positive growth, transformation, healing, joy, beauty, and new life.

Asking for God's blessing can nurture hope and resilience. Calling our attention to arenas of life where God is active and bringing new life provides another way of praising and thanking God. When people see and name God at work, it helps liberate them from quagmires of grief, shame, and despair that can shield them from experiencing love, joy, and meaning. In worship, a leader could use this form of prayer as the pastoral prayer, opening and leaving space for voiced response from the congregation. Similarly, this could be a prayer activity for a Sunday school class, a family, or small group. This prayer activates participants, engaging their agency in actively asking God for blessing and intervention in our lives and broader world.

This prayer practice may also be useful as a personal journaling prompt, with families, or small groups. I have experimented with this prayer in worship class with students asking God to bless and intervene in our lives and world. I found this type of prayer to be most effective when participants had some introduction to the prayer and time to reflect. Students suggested that it made for a fruitful journaling prompt for those who are nurtured by having time and space to prayerfully reflect before participating in a public prayer. If a leader would choose to use this in public worship, it would be helpful to offer some written words of instruction in advance and practice it for a season to allow for full participation. My words framing the prayer were as follows:

> God of truth, mercy, justice, and peace. Stir our hearts and minds so that we are moved by the things that move you. There is so much in our world that does not honor you and your intentions for creation. God, we ask for you to intervene in these situations and circumstances. (*Open space for participants to ask for God's intervention.*)
>
> And yet God, we also see and celebrate your presence in our world, we experience your love. We ask for your continued blessing upon these experiences and events that reflect you. (*Open space for participants to ask for God's continued blessing.*)
>
> We thank you God for your active presence in our lives and world; we ask that you help us participate in that which you bless. Give us courage to care, to engage, and to intervene in your name in those circumstances that do not reflect your desires for your creation. Bless this time together we pray. Amen.

Blessing as a physical experience

Bodily actions frequently accompany blessing in worship and other settings. At the end of worship, a pastor or leader may raise her or his arms to extend God's blessing over the people. In more individual acts, God's blessing may involve laying a hand on another's head or arm or making the sign of the cross on another person's forehead or hand, sometimes with oil, for example in a healing service or during an ordination. In some traditions, people cross themselves as a sign of blessing. These acts can be powerfully formative, part of our individual and collective muscle memory over time.

Jesus' incarnate presence among us demonstrates the ways that God uses physical experiences and materials in our world to bless us. Jesus' experience of baptism was a blessing, Jesus' feeding and healing ministries attended to physical needs. The risen Christ blessed his disciples.

Because we are embodied, it makes sense to pay attention to physical actions and prayerful postures that accompany the experience of God's blessing, and to experiment with what may work best in different settings. Doing physical acts together as an assembly of the faithful can help to regulate the nervous system during seasons of intense traumatic stress. Singing, breathing and moving are all rhythmic and soothing actions. Incorporating or embracing physical actions to receiving blessings can be restorative to communities.

Kneeling is one example of a receptive posture to experience blessing. In my own Mennonite tradition, footwashing is a potent act that can carry with it a sense of the participants being agents of the Holy Spirit in an act of mutual blessing and mutual service, following Jesus' teaching in the gospel of John. Footwashing involves kneeling before another, taking on a vulnerable posture of love and care. My own experience of believer's baptism in a Mennonite setting involved kneeling while water was poured over my head.

Holding one's hands open similarly may demonstrate a receptive posture. This posture is often the one from which we receive communion and may be helpful for receiving any blessing in worship.

Blessing as giving to others

In scripture, God's blessings do not stop with the recipient. There is a sense in which God's blessings are meant to inspire, grow, and extend the witness of God's love. In this sense a blessing is a bit like the "magic penny" in the children's song. When the magic penny is shared, it increases. In this way, blessing acts as a counterweight to forces of self-protection and fear of scarcity that drive so much behavior, particularly behavior during seasons of stress and trauma.

Sharing resources with others can be a form of extending God's blessing, bearing witness to the activity of the Holy Spirit here and now, and living into God's call to "be a blessing" in the world (Genesis 12:2–3). In the aftermath of trauma, there may be intensified material needs alongside the need to process trauma. When deadly tornados devastated parts of Kentucky weeks before Christmas 2021, the governor's wife, Britainy Beshear, established a toy drive for children who had been affected. The results were an unprecedented outpouring of donated toys and games coming to Kentucky from across the country. The governor's office reported more than two hundred thousand dollars in cash and gift cards, and hundreds of thousands of toys. The donations were enough to cover not only Christmas but also birthday presents for the coming year.[35]

Tammy McKinney's nine-year-old, Sammy, was just one of many children who lost their homes. For stressed and traumatized parents and broader communities, Christmas was one of many aspects of life that was completely upended. Uprooted and anxious children may have imagined that Santa couldn't deliver since their homes were destroyed. McKinney reflected, "He thought Santa Claus has forgot about us and I told him, 'No, he has not. He knows where we are all the time.'" She added, "You gotta do what you gotta do for kids, to make them a little bit more hopeful."[36]

Material giving to others is concrete and measurable. It can be a sign of God blessing and intervening on behalf of those who are suffering. Amidst the chronic suffering of COVID-19, individuals and groups can easily become overwhelmed. It seems that we cannot resolve any issue, so we cease trying. We can be tempted to look away and cultivate numb stoicism as a means of conserving energy. People cannot prevent tornados, completely avoid their destructive power, or turn back time to a world before COVID, but we can do something. Donating toys, books, games, and money became an act of the Holy Spirit, addressing physical, emotional, and spiritual needs in survivors of the tornados and restoring agency within the broader community.

Blessing as compassionate witness

Acts of compassionate witness can bear some resemblance to giving to others following a traumatic event. But this category of "blessing-in-action" is broader and more elastic in interpretation and practice.

In May of 2019, a cluster of powerful tornados struck Dayton, Ohio. The tornados brought the worst damage in neighborhoods that were already economically distressed. Everyone in the community was shaken by traumatic stress.

In the aftermath of the tornados, there were many opportunities to give concrete items to those who had lost their homes. Our community center set out barrels for socks, diapers, and bottled water. Accounts were set up to manage monetary donations. The local schools engaged in food drives. Schools and libraries opened to the public as day shelters where people could get snacks and water and charge their phones. Teams of people drove in from surrounding areas to pick up debris in the hardest hit neighborhoods.

These instinctual actions directed towards easing the pain of others also have a beneficial impact on the one offering the act of service or care. Kaethe Weingarten describes these responses as acts of "compassionate witness." When done with intention, these concrete acts of blessing can help to ease traumatic stress.

Weingarten's invitation to engage in acts of compassionate witness arises in response to what she calls "common shock," acts of violence and violation that we witness every day.[37] This morning as I got ready, news of war in Ukraine dominated headlines. I listened to a heartbreaking report of civilians killed in a bombardment after venturing out from a makeshift bomb shelter in a parking garage to get bottled water. The reporter described gruesome wounds and bottles of water scattered around bodies. When I dropped my son off to catch the school bus, the driver yelled at a child who accidentally smeared a window blowing kisses to her mom. The child responded with tears. These situations are not directly part of my personal life, but they affect me. Any additional events of brokenness and violence that I witness on top of the chronic stress of COVID feels like a difficult burden.

Weingarten points out that we experience situations like this every day. This is common shock because it happens *all the time* and we hold the impact *collectively,* in common.[38] Typically we stifle the responses to these indirect, glancing blows of violence and violation and we become what she names "toxic witnesses." Those who see but do nothing, we stuff down the pain, shut our mouths, avert our gaze, and numb emotional responses.

My own biggest "aha" moment in studying trauma has come in recognizing that I have a choice when I experience common shock. I can choose to listen to my body, heart, mind, and spirit and attend to resonant pain that arises when another is hurt. The other need not be another human being to elicit this response. Indeed, we feel the pain when any part of God's beloved creation experiences harm and suffering.

The practice of compassionate witnessing allows us to attend to the pain in such a way that we can stay present while also continuing to live and move forward. Concrete responses can be symbolic or address a need at the locus of pain. Compassionate witnessing can happen with individuals or groups.

Writing blessings can be a form of compassionate witness. Creating a blessing can be an act that attends to the locus of the pain as well as the collateral common shock pain experienced by others at varying levels.

Medical and frontline workers have experienced the pandemic with unique intensity that contributes to our collective stress. One study suggests that 20 percent of medical workers may be suffering from PTSD.[39] My brother is a chaplain at a hospital in a large city. I lack words to adequately express his experience of caregiving in the midst of COVID-19. The pain, loss, suffering, and trauma were immense among all who were touched in the medical ecosystem, from patients and families to medical staff and other hospital caregivers such as chaplains and social workers. Conversations with my brother have often sparked a sense of common shock within me.

One example of a story that begged a response of compassionate witness involved the death of an undocumented man from COVID. The man had stayed at the hospital for more than a year in varying degrees of suffering and decline. He was unable to be released into any other kind of care because he was undocumented. After death, his body remained in the morgue for months, which was upsetting to staff who had come to care deeply for him. A funeral home with a contract to attend to unclaimed deaths from COVID took the body and cremated it, but it remains unclaimed. The remains will likely be scattered in a place for unclaimed people. After a couple of months in prayer and reflection, I invited my brother to create a written testimony or case study of his experience with this man. We felt that writing the story down constituted a first level of compassionate witness. We removed any identifying information to protect the dignity of the man and his family.

I shared the story with a group of clergy. After prayer and reflection, we created prayers of lament for the death and the dehumanizing circumstances and systems that added to his suffering. We created prayers of blessing for the man, his family, and the hospital staff who cared for him. Prayer is a spiritual act of compassionate witness that an individual or group can take when no other action is possible.

Blessing as a transitional guide

Earlier in the chapter I described the gift of my colleague's blessing after I announced my transition to another seminary. Transitions of all kinds can be difficult and trigger traumatic responses—even if the occasion is "happy." Ritual helps us move through a situation that feels strange and gives us guidance, such as a blessing on the occasion of retirement, a wedding, or a funeral.

In the aftermath of trauma, transitions can be especially challenging. The traumatic stress of the pandemic has created extra emotional transitional freight for many. In a happy moment, we may feel deep grief for a loved one who is not present. We may feel anger for earlier missed milestones. Students who missed their high school commencement celebrations may feel grief at commencement from university.

Anniversaries of weddings that occurred in limited and highly constrained circumstances may carry a painful edge alongside joy. This experience is not new to anyone who has experienced loss, trauma, or grief, but the scale of loss related to COVID means that we need greater awareness.

At the time of this writing, over one million people have died from COVID in the United States. If each of those losses impacts just ten others, we have ten million friends, family members, and neighbors potentially facing increased grief amidst transitions.

Part of the challenge of traumatic response is that we can feel stuck amid traumatic responses and at a loss for words. Blessings can give us language to help us attend to pain and grief and engage with life in meaningful ways.

We regularly offer blessings at the end of worship and other gatherings and when members move away from our communities. Leaders may wish to extend a blessing for other transitions as well, such as starting school, graduation, retirement, leaving and starting a new job, or a local move to a new home or nursing care facility. Blessings may be written by a leader or could be written by a care group. In the context of worship, blessings may be sung.

*   *   *

Blessings can offer comfort and love in times of transition and struggle. Blessings can be opportunities for congregations and groups to name God's presence in our world, to process trauma and seek God's healing. However, care needs to be taken to not collapse blessings into material transactions. Our understanding of blessing is formed by the work and person of Jesus Christ, so at times we may experience blessing as hidden in the cross.

God's gift of sacraments may offer a helpful reference point for unpacking blessings. Blessings are a sign of God's overflowing and deeply intentional love poured out on creation. Blessings are a sign of the resurrection and bear witness to God's life-giving intentions for creation as present here and now. Looking for and naming signs and instances of God's action in our world is a powerful spiritual practice that builds resilience and hope.

Reflecting on healing and resilience in relationship to trauma can kindle a primal desire, a longing to live in such a way that trauma, violence, and pain in our world might be lessened. Sometimes this can be difficult to imagine. One of the ways that sin and brokenness works in our world is to blind us to God's redemptive presence when we need it most. As I complete this book, our nation is deep in grief and mired in anger after two mass shootings: a racially motivated attack targeting Black shoppers in a grocery store in Buffalo, New York, and another by a troubled and hurting young man who unleashed his rage, murdering children and teachers sheltering in their classrooms in Uvalde, Texas.

After the shooting in Uvalde, blood banks issued a request for donations. Mass casualty events often elicit increased need for blood, and Texas was already experiencing shortages. Within hours, donors showed up, driven by a desire to do something to extend themselves toward those who were suffering from trauma, grief, and immeasurable loss. Funeral directors and lawyers in the area offered their services for free and monetary donations poured in to help grieving families.[40] These acts are instinctual acts of compassionate witness, marks of resilience and signs of resurrection life.

The practices of lament, storytelling, and blessing are tools that can unlock and support resilience in individuals and groups. When they operate in concert, there can be a dynamic interplay that reflects a holistic life of faith and a maturing relationship with God that can sanctify our imaginations and our lives, so that we might begin to see God at work in our world and bear witness, embodying what we long for most.

> *A Blessing for Pastors and Leaders*
> May the Spirit who kindled your call sustain you.
> May the love of Jesus surround you in your holy work.
> May God wipe away your tears, attend to your wounds,
>   and give you faith, courage, capacity, and hope, enough
>   for each moment,
> that you might experience New Creation even here,
>   even now.
> Amen.

Acknowledgments

This book was conceived, gestated, and birthed during the difficult season in which our world has struggled in the grip of COVID-19 and many accompanying crises. I am thankful for the rich resiliency network in my life. The stress of this season deepens my gratefulness for those who love me and supported this project.

I am thankful to United Theological Seminary. I thank my faculty colleagues, Dean David Watson, President Kent Millard, and the Board of Trustees for their encouragement in the form of a sabbatical to focus on writing. I thank my students, particularly in the 2022 Work of Worship class, for experimenting with some of the ideas in the book.

I wish to thank Fairmont Presbyterian Church, who provided me a safe and quiet space for research and writing when my home was noisy with children and spouse working at home and my favorite writing spots were closed due to the pandemic. I am grateful to the pastoral team for fruitful conversation, particularly Brian Maguire, who offered encouragement and generously shared prayers and sermons. My life and this book are richer for these relationships.

I am grateful for many conversation partners. Thank you to my friends in the Lower Susquehanna Synod of the ELCA, Richard Jorgensen, Marsha Roscoe, Bishop James Dunlop, and clergy participants in the Bishops Convocation and certificate program in trauma-aware preaching. Thank you to Tom Boomershine for conversation around biblical storytelling, to Dick and Elise Eslinger for your ongoing friendship and insights particularly in worship, and to Casey Barton for numerous theological discussions by text. Thank you to Bob Howard for pointing me to a key resource early on, to UM Bishop Gregory Palmer and MC USA Central District Conference Minister Doug Luginbill for providing me opportunities and venues to share ideas with clergy, and to the participants in my workshops at Princeton Theological Seminary's Engle Institute of Preaching in 2021 and 2022.

I am thankful for the friendship and wisdom of Paul Wilson. I can't imagine my life without Paul's influence. His insights, keen editorial eye, and pastor's heart greatly improved this book.

Thank you to the editors and team at Herald Press. It means a great deal to me to publish with a Mennonite press and to work with a team with shared history and commitments. Thank you to Sara Versluis and Laura Leonard for your encouragement and editing skills and to Amy Gingerich for supporting this project.

Finally, I thank my spouse Steve, children Maggie and Teddy, and my dear friend Emily Rodgers for their patience and love and for distractions and levity that offered much-needed balance amidst writing and researching about trauma. Steve has listened and offered feedback all along the way with his customary good humor.

Notes

INTRODUCTION

1. Brené Brown, *Atlas of the Heart: Mapping Meaningful Connection and the Language of Human Experience* (New York: Random House, 2021), xxii.
2. Quoted in Kat Lonsdorf, "People Are Developing Trauma Like Symptoms as the Pandemic Wears On," NPR, April 7, 2022, https://www.npr.org/2022/04/07/1087195915/covid-pandemic-trauma-mentalhealth.
3. Resmaa Menakem, *My Grandmother's Hands: Racialized Trauma and the Pathway to Mending Our Hearts and Bodies* (Las Vegas: Central Recovery Press, 2017), 19–20. I explore this idea further in chapter 2.
4. Ed Prideaux, "How to Heal the 'Mass Trauma' of COVID-19," BBC, February 3, 2021, https://www.bbc.com/future/article/20210203-after-the-covid-19-pandemic-how-will-we-heal/.

CHAPTER 1

1. Melissa Fay Greene, "How Will We Remember the Pandemic? The Science of How Our Memories Form—and How They Shape Our Future," *The Atlantic*, May 2021, 60.
2. Throughout this book, the terms *tragic events* or *circumstances*, *crises/crisis*, *traumatic stress* or *stressor*, *traumatic event*—or *traumagenic event*—and *ongoing experiences* are used interchangeably to describe situations or events that may lead to a stress-based traumatic response.

3. Kai Erikson, *A New Species of Trouble: The Human Experience of Modern Disasters* (New York: Norton, 1995), 228, 230, 231.

4. Collective trauma is also called "mass trauma" in some literature.

5. Ed Prideaux, "How to Heal the 'Mass Trauma' of COVID-19," BBC, February 3, 2021, https://www.bbc.com/future/article/20210203-after-the-covid-19-pandemic-how-will-we-heal/.

6. Kyle Pearce, "Fractals in Nature: Develop Your Pattern Recognition Skills in the Forest," DIY Genius, November 4, 2018, https://www.diygenius.com/fractals-in-nature/.

7. Adrienne Maree Brown, *Emergent Strategy: Shaping Change, Changing Worlds* (Chico, CA: AK Press, 2017), 51–52.

8. Erikson, *New Species of Trouble*, 231. See also Kate Wiebe, "Toward a Faith-Based Approach to Healing after Collective Trauma," in *Tragedies and Christian Congregations: The Practical Theology of Trauma*, Megan Warner, Christopher Southgate, Carla A. Grosche-Miller, and Hilary Ison (New York: Routledge, 2019), 70. Wiebe's interpretation of Erikson's work provides a helpful faith perspective.

9. Erikson, *New Species of Trouble*, 233.

10. The concept of collective trauma can also be a challenging one, not without its critics who feel that it erases difference and highlights a particular narrative arc that moves towards resilience as an acceptable destination rather than other very common expressions of trauma, which are less tidy. Not everyone within a particular collective experiences a traumatic event in the same way. Is there a particular path for nurturing collective resilience in the face of traumatic events that impact larger groups of people? Indeed, Nicholas Stargardt notes, "There is a limit to the number of occasions a whole society can stop and engage in rituals of commemoration and soul-searching." See Nicholas Stargardt, "A German Trauma? The Experience of the Second World War in Germany," in *Enduring Trauma through the Life Cycle*, ed. Eileen McGinley and Arturo Varchevker (London: Taylor and Francis, 2013), 174–76.

11. Erikson, *New Species of Trouble*, 232.

12. Peter Felix Kellermann, *Sociodrama and Collective Trauma* (London: Jessica Kingsley Publishers, 2007), 44. Like other traumatic responses, these stages tend to be stable across different cultures.

13. Kellermann, 37.

14. Wiebe, "Toward a Faith-Based Approach," 68. This sense of basic trust is a key feature of attachment theory.
15. Wiebe, 68; see also Erikson, *New Species of Trouble*, 228.
16. Wiebe, 69.
17. Wiebe, 68.
18. Kellermann, *Sociodrama and Collective Trauma*, 43.
19. Ann Marie Fleming (director and screenwriter), *I Was a Child of Holocaust Survivors*, National Film Board of Canada, 2010. Based on Bernice Eisenstein, *I Was a Child of Holocaust Survivors* (Toronto: McClelland and Stewart, 2007).
20. Wiebe, "Toward a Faith-Based Approach," 66.
21. Erikson, *New Species of Trouble*, 237. See also Wiebe, "Toward a Faith-Based Approach," 70.
22. Wiebe, "Toward a Faith-Based Approach," 70. See also Erikson, 237.
23. Wiebe, 71; Erikson, 233.
24. Wiebe, 71; Erikson, 236.
25. Erikson, 236.
26. Joseph Singer, Nadia Sussman, Nina Martin, and Akilah Johnson, "Black Men Have the Shortest Lifespans of Any Americans. This Theory Helps Explain Why," ProPublica, December 20, 2020, https://www.propublica.org/article/black-men-have-the-shortest-lifespans-of-any-americans-this-theory-helps-explain-why. See also Sherman A. James, "John Henryism and the Health of African-Americans," *Culture, Medicine & Psychiatry* 18, no. 2 (June 1994): 163, doi:10.1007/BF01379448.
27. APM Research Lab Staff, "The Color of Coronavirus: COVID-19 Deaths by Race and Ethnicity in the U.S.," APM Research Lab, January 7, 2021, https://www.apmresearchlab.org/covid/deaths-by-race.
28. Clifford Geertz, *The Interpretation of Cultures* (Basic Books, 1973), 4–5.
29. Mary de Young, "Collective Trauma: Insights from a Research Errand," American Academy of Experts in Traumatic Stress, accessed January 8, 2021, https://www.aaets.org/traumatic-stress-library/collective-trauma-insights-from-a-research-errand.
30. Jeffrey C. Alexander, "Toward a Theory of Cultural Trauma," in Jeffrey C. Alexander, Ron Eyerman, Bernard Giesen, Neil J. Smelser, and Piotr Sztompka, *Cultural Trauma and Collective Identity* (Berkeley, CA: University of California Press,

2004), 1. Digital resource accessed January 14, 2021, https://doi
.org/10.1525/9780520936768.

31. Quoted in Mary Carole McCauley, "With New Book, Madeleine
Albright Sheds Light on Long-Hidden Family Secrets," *Baltimore
Sun*, May 5, 2012, https://www.baltimoresun.com/entertainment/
arts/bs-ae-albright-pratt-20120505-story.html.

32. De Young, "Collective Trauma."

33. De Young.

34. De Young.

35. Resmaa Menakem, *My Grandmother's Hands: Racialized Trauma
and the Pathway to Mending Our Hearts and Bodies* (Las Vegas:
Central Recovery Press, 2017), 37–40.

36. Erikson, *New Species of Trouble*, 29.

37. Stephen Lepore and Tracey Revenson, "Resilience and Post-
Traumatic Growth: Recovery, Resistance, and Reconfiguration,"
in *Handbook of Posttraumatic Growth: Research and
Practice*, ed. Lawrence G. Calhoun and Richard G. Tedeschi
(New York: Psychology Press, 2014), 24, 25–27, https://doi.
org/10.4324/9781315805597.

38. Anna Weiner, "Looking Back at an Unimaginable Year," *New
Yorker Radio Hour*, December 25, 2020.

39. Weiner.

40. Lepore and Revenson, "Resilience and Post-Traumatic Growth,"
25.

41. Lepore and Revenson, 26.

42. Tonya Mosley and Allison Hagan, "Indigenous Researcher
Transforms Body Bag into a Healing Ribbon Dress," *Here and
Now*, April 20, 2021.

43. Cecilia Nowell, "They Asked for PPE and Got Body Bags Instead—
She Turned Them into a Healing Dress," *Vogue*, February 4, 2021,
https://www.vogue.com/article/body-bag-native-ribbon-dress. See
close-up image.

44. Lepore and Revenson, "Resilience and Post-Traumatic Growth,"
27. Reconfiguration can sometimes be aligned with understandings
of post-traumatic growth (PTG), which will be discussed later in
this chapter.

45. Thomas Hübl, *Healing Collective Trauma: A Process for
Integrating Our Intergenerational and Cultural Wounds* (Boulder,
CO: Sounds True, 2020), xvi.

46. De Young, "Collective Trauma."

47. De Young.

48. Alexander, "Toward a Theory of Cultural Trauma," 1.

49. Nati Garicia, "Every Child Matters," Cultural Survival, September 29, 2021, https://www.culturalsurvival.org/news/orange-shirt-day-uncovering-dark-history-residential-schools-canada.

50. Government of Canada, "National Day for Truth and Reconciliation," September 29, 2021, https://www.canada.ca/en/canadian-heritage/campaigns/national-day-truth-reconciliation.html.

51. Alexander, "Toward a Theory of Cultural Trauma," 1.

52. Avishai Margalit, *On Betrayal* (Cambridge, MA: Harvard University Press, 2017), 263–64.

53. For more information, see https://www.valleyopendoors.org/. When the incidents described took place, Open Doors was known as HARTS (Harrisonburg and Rockingham Thermal Shelter.) The story is based on my husband's memories of working with HARTS as a pastor in Harrisonburg.

54. Margalit, *On Betrayal*, 263–64.

55. Leonard Cohen, "Anthem," *The Future*, Columbia, 1992.

56. Laurence G. Calhoun and Richard G. Tedeschi, "The Foundations of Posttraumatic Growth: An Expanded Framework," in *Handbook of Posttraumatic Growth: Research and Practice*, ed. L. G. Calhoun and R. G. Tedeschi (New York: Routledge, 2006), 4.

57. Calhoun and Tedeschi, "Foundations of Posttraumatic Growth," 5–6, 11.

58. Kate Bowler, "It's Okay to Laugh," September 24, 2019, in *Everything Happens with Kate Bowler*, podcast, https://katebowler.com/podcasts/.

59. Shelly Rambo, *Resurrecting Wounds: Living in the Afterlife of Trauma* (Waco, TX: Baylor UP, 2017), 42, 105.

60. Rambo, 147.

61. Alex Bierman, "Does Religion Buffer the Effects of Discrimination on Mental Health? Differing Effects by Race," *Journal for the Scientific Study of Religion* 45, no. 4 (2006): 551–65, http://www.jstor.org/stable/4621935; Christopher G. Ellison, Reed T. DeAngelis, and Metin Güven, "Does Religious Involvement Mitigate the Effects of Major Discrimination on the Mental Health of African Americans? Findings from the Nashville Stress and Health Study," *Religions* 8, no. 9 (2017): 195.

CHAPTER 2

1. Chris Cameron, "Memorial along National Mall Offers Stark Reminder of Virus's Toll," *New York Times*, September 17, 2021, accessed September 27, 2021, https://www.nytimes.com/2021/09/17/us/politics/national-mall-covid-deaths.html.
2. Michel Martin, "Visitors See More Than Just Grief and Loss at COVID-19 Memorial in D.C.," NPR, September 26, 2021, https://www.npr.org/2021/09/26/1040791827/visitors-see-more-than-just-grief-and-loss-at-covid-19-memorial-in-d-c.
3. Cameron, "Memorial along National Mall."
4. Ed Yong, "How Did This Many Deaths Become Normal?" *The Atlantic*, March 8, 2022, https://www.theatlantic.com/health/archive/2022/03/covid-us-death-rate/626972/.
5. Samantha Balaban, "It Used to Be Just a Fence. It Became a Tribute to Things Lost and Found in 2020," NPR, December 26, 2020, https://www.npr.org/2020/12/26/949556139/it-used-to-be-just-a-fence-it-became-a-tribute-to-things-lost-and-found-in-2020.
6. Ed Yong, "What Happens When Americans Can Finally Exhale," *The Atlantic*, May 20, 2021, https://www.theatlantic.com/health/archive/2021/05/pandemic-trauma-summer/618934/.
7. Brené Brown, *Atlas of the Heart: Mapping Meaningful Connection and the Language of Human Experience* (New York: Random House, 2021), 84.
8. W. Derek Suderman, "The Cost of Losing Lament for the Community of Faith: On Brueggemann, Ecclesiology, and the Social Audience of Prayer," *Journal of Theological Interpretation* 6, no. 2 (2012): 201–18.
9. Nancy L. Duff, "Recovering Lamentation as a Practice in the Church," in *Lament: Reclaiming Practices in Pew, Pulpit, and Public Square* (Louisville: Westminster John Knox, 2005), 3.
10. Walter Brueggemann, "The Costly Loss of Lament," *Journal for the Study of the Old Testament* 6 (1986): 57–71, 62.
11. Nancy C. Lee, "Lament in the Bible and in Music and Poetry across Cultures Today," SBL Teaching the Bible e-newsletter, August 3, 2012, https://www.sbl-site.org/assets/pdfs/TB7_Lamentmusic_NL.pdf.
12. Walter Brueggemann, "From Hurt to Joy, From Death to Life," *Interpretation* 28, no. 1 (January 1974): 5–8.
13. Brueggemann, "From Hurt to Joy," 8.
14. Brueggemann, 9.
15. Lee, "Lament in the Bible."

16. Anne E. Streaty Wimberly, "Religious Education and Lament: Inviting Cries from the Hearth, Guiding the Way Forward," in *From Lament to Advocacy: Black Religious Education and Public Ministry*, ed. Anne E. Streaty Wimberly, Nathaniel D. West, and Annie Lockhart-Gilroy (Nashville: Wesley's Foundery Books, 2020), 17.

17. Wimberly, 18.

18. CBS News, "MLK Assassination: How Walter Cronkite Covered the April 4, 1968 Tragedy," April 4, 2018, accessed September 16, 2021, https://www.cbsnews.com/news/mlk-assassination-walter-cronkite-report-cbs-evening-news-broadcast-april-4-1968/.

19. Wimberly, "Religious Education and Lament," 18, 19.

20. A. Elaine Crawford, *Hope in the Holler: A Womanist Theology* (Louisville: Westminster John Knox, 2002), xii, cited in Wimberly, "Religious Education and Lament," 19.

21. Wimberly, "Religious Education and Lament," 19.

22. I have permission to share this story.

23. Howard Thurman, *Jesus and the Disinherited* (Boston: Beacon Press, 1996), 36, cited in Wimberly, "Religious Education and Lament," 19.

24. Thomas Gibbons-Neff and Natalia Yermack, "Traces of Lives Cut Short: Bread on a Park Bench, Blood Pooled Nearby," *New York Times*, April 6, 2022, https://www.nytimes.com/2022/04/06/world/europe/ukraine-kharkiv-death.html.

25. Wimberly, "Religious Education and Lament," 20. Wimberly draws on Howard Thurman's phrase.

26. Wimberly, 20. See also Mychal Denzel Smith, "The Rebirth of Black Rage," *The Nation*, August 13, 2015, 7, www.thenation.com/article/archive/the-rebirth-of-Black-rage/.

27. Suderman, "Cost of Losing Lament."

28. Suderman, 202; see also Walter Brueggemann, "The Costly Loss of Lament." Suderman pulls from Westermann, who notes that the one with whom a lamenter may have complaint may be in the crowd of those who listen to the lament. See Claus Westermann, *Praise and Lament in the Psalms*, trans. Keith R. Crim and Richard N. Soulen (Atlanta: John Knox, 1981), 169.

29. Suderman, "Cost of Losing Lament," 204–6.

30. Suderman, 209, 211.

31. Suderman, 213.

32. Thomas Long, "Troubled?," sermon housed on archives of Calvin Theological Seminary's Center for Excellence in

Preaching, accessed May 24, 2021, http://cep.calvinseminary.edu/audio-sermon-archives/#ss.

33. Kaethe Weingarten, *Common Shock: Witnessing Violence Every Day* (New York: Dutton, 2003). Chapter 4 of this book goes into greater detail on Weingarten's work and the potential for congregational practices.

34. N. T. Wright, "Christianity Offers No Answers about the Coronavirus. It's Not Supposed To," *Time*, March 29, 2020.

35. Wimberly, "Religious Education and Lament," 2–3.

36. Kate Bowler's podcast *Everything Happens* acknowledges this dynamic at the start of each episode. Chapter 3 of this book unpacks the potential of narrative to shape experiences of trauma and resilience in greater detail.

37. Kate Bowler, podcast introduction and newest book, *No Cure for Being Human (And Other Truths I Need to Hear)* (New York: Random House, 2021).

38. Kate Bowler, "Introduction," in *Everything Happens with Kate Bowler*, podcast, accessed March 19, 2021, https://katebowler.com/podcasts/.

39. Leonard Cohen, "Anthem," *The Future*, Columbia, 1992.

40. William Blaine-Wallace, *When Tears Sing: The Art of Lament in Christian Community* (Maryknoll, NY: Orbis, 2020), 10.

41. Resmaa Menakem, *My Grandmother's Hands: Racialized Trauma and the Pathway to Mending Our Hearts and Bodies* (Las Vegas: Central Recovery Press, 2017), 19–20.

42. In *Spirit Speech: Lament and Celebration in Preaching* (Nashville: Abingdon, 2009), Luke Powery reminds preachers to balance celebration with lament. The dynamic of trouble or human need and grace serve as a deep theological grammar that drives Paul Scott Wilson's approach to preaching in *The Four Pages of the Sermon*, rev. ed. (Nashville: Abingdon, 2018).

43. Brueggemann, "Costly Loss of Lament," 61.

44. Walter Brueggemann, *Israel's Praise: Doxology against Idolatry and Ideology* (Philadelphia: Fortress, 1988), 140.

45. *West Wing* episode "Two Cathedrals," 2001.

46. June F. Dickie, "The Importance of Lament in Pastoral Ministry: Biblical Basis and Some Applications," *Verbum et Ecclesia* 40, no. 1 (2002): 3–4.

47. Mathew Wilcoxen "The Practice of Lament," *Conversatio Divina*, April 10, 2020, https://conversatio.org/classroom/the-practice-of-lament/.

48. Wilcoxen.

49. Brueggemann, *Israel's Praise*, 141.

50. Brueggemann, "Costly Loss of Lament," 59.

51. John Witvliet, "The Cumulative Power of Transformation in Public Worship: Cultivating Gratitude and Expectance for the Holy Spirit's Work," in *Worship That Changes Lives: Multidisciplinary and Congregational Perspectives on Spiritual Transformation*, ed. Alexis D. Abernathy (Grand Rapids: Baker, 2008), 44, emphasis in original.

52. Walter Brueggemann, *Israel's Praise*, 133.

53. Don Saliers, *Worship as Theology: Foretaste of Divine Glory* (Nashville: Abingdon, 1994), 121.

54. Katie Mansfield, comp. *STAR Level 2 Workbook* (Harrisonburg, VA: Eastern Mennonite University, 2021), 78.

55. Dickie, "Lament in Pastoral Ministry," 5.

56. Larry Smith, "The Pandemic in Six-Word Memoir," *New York Times*, September 11, 2020, https://www.nytimes.com/2020/09/11/opinion/coronavirus-pandemic-poetry-memoirs.html.

57. Brian Maguire, "A Prayer of Lament for the People of Ukraine," Beside Still Waters, weekly congregational email newsletter, Fairmont Presbyterian Church, Kettering, Ohio, March 8, 2022. Reprinted with permission.

58. Dickie, "Lament in Pastoral Ministry," 4.

59. This is attributed to Augustine without specific reference. Brian Wren, *Praying Twice: The Music and Words of Congregational Song* (Louisville: Westminster John Knox, 2000), 1.

60. Bessel van der Kolk, *The Body Keeps the Score: Brain, Mind, and Body in the Healing of Trauma* (New York: Penguin, 2014), 43–44. See also Joni S. Sancken, *Words That Heal: Preaching Hope to Wounded Souls* (Nashville: Abingdon, 2019), 80–81.

61. See Thomas touching Jesus' wounds in John 20:26–28.

62. Dickie, "Lament in Pastoral Ministry," 5.

63. Dickie.

64. Dickie includes a similar set of questions, 5.

65. Dickie, 8.

66. Martin Luther King Jr., "Letter from a Birmingham Jail," in *A Testament of Hope: The Essential Writings and Speeches of Martin Luther King Jr.*, ed. James M. Washington (San Francisco: Harper San Francisco, 1986), 290.

67. "The Psalm with a Painful Lament— Psalm 13," Calvin Institute of Christian Worship, June 1, 2005,

https://worship.calvin.edu/resources/resource-library/
the-psalm-with-a-painful-lament-psalm-13/.
68. Powery, *Spirit Speech.*
69. James F. Kay, "The Word of the Cross at the Turn of the Ages,"
Interpretation: A Journal of Bible and Theology 53, no. 1 (1999):
44–56.
70. Points 1 to 6 are drawn from Powery, *Spirit Speech*, 119–23.
Powery writes from an African American perspective and examples
in the book reflect that context, but his observations can be
contextualized more broadly.
71. Sally Brown, "When Lament Shapes the Sermon," in *Lament:
Reclaiming Practices in Pulpit, Pew, and Public Square*, ed. Sally
Brown and Patrick Miller (Louisville: Westminster John Knox,
2005), 28.
72. Wilson, *Four Pages of the Sermon.*
73. Brown, "Lament Shapes the Sermon," 29.
74. I have Maggie's permission to share this story.
75. Sumathi Reddy, "Eating Disorders Surged among Adolescents
in Pandemic," *Wall Street Journal*, June 21, 2021, https://www.
wsj.com/articles/eating-disorders-surged-among-adolescents-in-
pandemic-11624302000; Benedict Carey, "For Some Teens, It's
Been a Year of Anxiety and Trips to the E.R.," *New York Times*,
February 23, 2021.

CHAPTER 3

1. Anna Kaplan, "Sales of 'Maus' Soar 753% in Last Week of January
Following Ban by Tennessee School District," *Forbes*, February
4, 2022, https://www.forbes.com/sites/annakaplan/2022/02/04/
sales-of-maus-soar-753-in-last-week-of-january-following-ban-by-
tennessee-school-district/.
2. Tamim Ansary, "A Story of Us?," February 3, 2022, in *Throughline*,
podcast, https://www.npr.org/2022/02/02/1077733601/a-story-of-us.
3. Véronique Tadjo, *The Shadow of Imana* (Long Grove, IL:
Waveland Press, 2015), 11.
4. Stephen Crites, "The Narrative Quality of Experience," in *Why
Narrative? Readings in Narrative Theology*, ed. Gregory Jones and
Stanley Hauerwas (Eugene, OR: Wipf and Stock, 1997), 71.
5. Crites, 66.
6. Kate Bowler, "Nicole Chung: Family Lore," March 15, 2021,
in *Everything Happens with Kate Bowler*, podcast, https://
katebowler.com/podcasts/nicole-chung-family-lore/.

7. Judith Herman, *Trauma and Recovery: The Aftermath of Violence—from Domestic Abuse to Political Terror* (New York: Basic, 1992), 3.

8. Amy-Jill Levine, *Short Stories by Jesus: The Enigmatic Parables of a Controversial Rabbi* (New York: Harper One, 2014), 1–3.

9. Levine, 3.

10. For this and the previous three points, see Levine, 133–34, 137.

11. Nikki Graf, "Mail-in DNA Tests Bring Surprises about Family History for Many Users," Pew Research Center, August 6, 2019, https://www.pewresearch.org/fact-tank/2019/08/06/mail-in-dna-test-results-bring-surprises-about-family-history-for-many-users/.

12. Nora McInerny quoted in Kate Bowler, "It's Okay to Laugh," September 24, 2019, in *Everything Happens with Kate Bowler*, podcast, https://katebowler.com/podcasts/. McInerny and Bowler are discussing personal loss, but this is perhaps even more true in the experience of collective loss.

13. Laurence G. Calhoun and Richard G. Tedeschi, "The Foundations of Posttraumatic Growth: An Expanded Framework," in L. G. Calhoun and R. G. Tedeschi, eds., *Handbook of Posttraumatic Growth: Research and Practice*, 1st ed. (New York: Routledge, 2006), 4.

14. Chimamanda Ngozi Adiche, "The Danger of a Single Story," TED talk, TED Global 2009, July 2009, https://www.ted.com/talks/chimamanda_ngozi_adichie_the_danger_of_a_single_story#t-1101572.

15. Amanda Mull, "The Pandemic Has Erased Entire Categories of Friendship," *The Atlantic*, January 27, 2021, https://www.theatlantic.com/health/archive/2021/01/pandemic-goodbye-casual-friends/617839/.

16. Alan Kreider, *The Change of Conversion and the Origin of Christendom* (Eugene, OR: Wipf and Stock, 1999).

17. Kai Erikson, *A New Species of Trouble: The Human Experience of Modern Disasters* (New York: Norton, 1995), 242.

18. Calhoun and Tedeschi, "Foundations of Posttraumatic Growth," 5–6.

19. Joni S. Sancken, *Words That Heal: Preaching Hope to Wounded Souls* (Nashville: Abingdon, 2019), 13.

20. Frederic Luskin, *Forgive for Good: A Proven Prescription for Health and Happiness* (New York: Harper Collins, 2002), 36–38.

21. Luskin, *Forgive for Good*, 38.

22. Calhoun and Tedeschi, "Foundations of Posttraumatic Growth," 6.

23. Resmaa Menakem, *My Grandmother's Hands: Racialized Trauma and the Pathway to Mending Our Hearts and Bodies* (Las Vegas: Central Recovery Press, 2017), 165.

24. List inspired in part by Cathryn Wellner, "Seven Lessons," in *The Healing Heart for Communities: Storytelling for Strong and Healthy Communities*, ed. Allison M. Cox and David H. Albert (Gabriola Island, BC: New Society Publishers, 2003), 12–19.

25. Kurt Vonnegut, "Kurt Vonnegut Lecture" (lecture, Case Western Reserve, Cleveland, OH, February 4, 2004), https://www.youtube.com/watch?v=4_RUgnC1lm8. Also Kurt Vonnegut, cited in Ana Swanson, "Kurt Vonnegut Graphed the World's Most Popular Stories" *Washington Post*, February 9, 2015, https://www.washingtonpost.com/news/wonk/wp/2015/02/09/kurt-vonnegut-graphed-the-worlds-most-popular-stories/.

26. I am intentional about not using the phrase "moving on." A person never "moves on" from the loss of a loved one. We bring our loved one with us, but we can move forward and engage in the world of the living with hope and joy.

27. See also Shelly Rambo, *Resurrecting Wounds: Living in the Afterlife of Trauma* (Waco, TX: Baylor UP, 2017), 6.

28. Rambo, 6.

29. Rambo, 6. See also the work of Jürgen Moltmann, James Cone, Delores Williams, and Rosemary Radford Reuther.

30. Rambo, 5.

31. Richard Lischer, "The Limits of Story," *Interpretation* 38, no. 1 (January 1984): 26–38.

32. Practical theology, particularly homiletics, has a love affair with narrative; however, there are also strong cautions or critiques. Richard Lischer's germinal article on the limits of story remind us of the traumatic roots of Christian storytelling.

33. See also Herman, *Trauma and Recovery*, 158

34. David Brooks, "Some People Turn Suffering into Wisdom" *New York Times*, April 21, 2022, https://www.nytimes.com/2022/04/21/opinion/suffering-trauma-wisdom.html.

35. Brooks.

36. Brooks.

37. See chapter 2 and STAR Level 2 Workbook, 70. Model created by STAR team, updated in 2020. See also https://emu.edu/cjp/star/docs/snail-model.pdf. Accessed, June 28, 2022.

38. Luskin, *Forgive for Good*, 35.

39. Gene Knudsen Hoffman "An Enemy Is One Whose Story We Have Not Heard," *Fellowship, the Journal of the Fellowship of Reconciliation*, May/June 1997, accessed September 23, 2021, https://newconversations.net/communication-skills-library-of-articles-and-teaching-materials/gene-knudsen-hoffman-articles/an-enemy-is-one-whose-story-we-have-not-heard/.

40. Joni S. Sancken, Luke Powery, and John Rottman, *Getting to God: Preaching Good News in a Troubled World* (Eugene, OR: Cascade, forthcoming 2022); Maya Lou and Amy Wold, "Man Who Gunned Down Drug Informant Barry Seal in Baton Rouge Street Dies in Angola" *The Advocate*, September 2, 2015, accessed September 23, 2021, https://www.theadvocate.com/baton_rouge/news/crime_police/article_f09fb38d-4bb9-59ea-bda3-557497d84561.html

41. Sally A. Brown, *Sunday's Sermon for Monday's World : Preaching to Shape Daring Witness* (Grand Rapids: Eerdmans, 2020), 55–57.

42. Brown, 59.

43. Brown, 136–37, 138.

44. Thomas Boomershine, "Biblical Storytelling" (class lecture, United Theological Seminary, Dayton, OH, February 26, 2019); Thomas Boomershine, *Story Journey: An Invitation to the Gospel as Storytelling* (Nashville: Abingdon, 1988), 15, 67. I have Tom's permission to share his story.

45. Boomershine, *Story Journey*, 67.

46. Boomershine, 67.

47. See https://www.nbsint.org/.

48. Doug Lipman, "Games to Teach Interviewing," in *Healing Heart for Communities*, 138–40.

49. Language and discussion of using this material from conversation with Rev. Richard Jorgensen, director for Evangelical Mission for Renewing Mission, Lower Susquehanna Synod, November 4, 2021.

50. Diane Jacobson and Brenda Smith, *Story Matters: Naming, Claiming, and Living Our Biblical Identity* (Chicago: Evangelical Lutheran Church in America, 2017), 6–7.

51. Jacobson and Smith, 12.

52. Jacobson and Smith, 9.

53. See for example Larry Smith, "The Pandemic in Six-Word Memoir," *New York Times*, September 11, 2020, https://www.nytimes.com/2020/09/11/opinion/coronavirus-pandemic-poetry-memoirs.html.

54. Dennis Freeman, "The Wickenburg Way: A Storytelling History Play Unites a Community," in *Healing Heart for Communities*, 141–42.

CHAPTER 4

1. Photos by Angelica Edwards, Zayrha Rodriguez, "This Mother Wanted Her Son to Have Photos to Understand Her Breast Cancer Journey," NPR, October 31, 2021, accessed November 10, 2021, https://www.npr.org/sections/pictureshow/2021/10/31/1050548168/this-mother-wanted-her-son-to-hav-photos-to-understand-her-breast-cancer-journe.

2. Claus Westermann, *Blessing: In the Bible and the Life of the Church* (Philadelphia: Fortress Press, 1978), 104–5.

3. John O'Donohue, *To Bless the Space Between Us: A Book of Blessings* (New York: Doubleday, 2008), xiii.

4. Westermann, *Blessing*, 105.

5. Derek A. Rivard, *Blessing the World: Ritual and Lay Piety in Medieval Religion* (Baltimore: Catholic University of America Press, 2008), 25.

6. Westermann, *Blessing*, 3–4.

7. Rivard, *Blessing the World*, 25.

8. Westermann, *Blessing*, 4–5.

9. Rivard, *Blessing the World*, 26.

10. Rivard, 26–27. Rebekah's brothers bless her in Genesis 24:60; Isaac blesses Jacob in Genesis 27:27–29; and priests bless the people in Numbers 6:24–27.

11. Rivard, 29.

12. Rivard, 29.

13. Judith Herman, *Trauma and Recovery: The Aftermath of Violence—from Domestic Abuse to Political Terror* (New York: Basic Books, 1992), 3.

14. Brian Maguire, "Invoking Heaven" (sermon, Fairmont Presbyterian Church, Kettering, OH, September 9, 2021). Used with permission.

15. See Genesis 26 when Isaac digs new wells to avoid conflict and finds water; Isaiah 61:9 where the nations will see the progeny of Israel and see that they are blessed.

16. Christopher Wright Mitchell, *The Meaning of BRK "To Bless" in the Old Testament*, SBL Dissertation Series 95 (Atlanta: Society of Biblical Literature, 1987), 166.

17. Mitchell, *Meaning of BRK*, 166.

18. Mitchell, *Meaning of BRK*, 166.

19. Peter W. Marty, "If God Is Almighty, Why Do We Suffer?,"
    Christian Century, December 22, 2021, accessed January 4,
    2022, https://www.christiancentury.org/article/editorpublisher/
    if-god-almighty-why-do-we-suffer.

20. O'Donohue, *To Bless the Space*, xvi, 35.

21. Charles Taylor, *A Secular Age* (Cambridge, MA: Belknap Press of
    Harvard University Press, 2007).

22. These concepts are addressed in greater depth in chapter 2 of
    Joni S. Sancken, Luke Powery, and John Rottman, *Getting to God:
    Preaching Good News in a Troubled World* (Eugene, OR: Cascade,
    forthcoming 2022).

23. Laura Beres, "Celtic Spirituality: Exploring the Fascination
    across Time and Place," in *The Routledge Handbook of Religion,
    Spirituality and Social Work*, ed. B. Crisp (London: Routledge,
    2017), 101–2; Ian Bradley, *Pilgrimage: A Spiritual and Cultural
    Journey* (Oxford: Lion, 2010), 108.

24. Sancken, Powery, and Rottman, *Getting to God*.

25. Sancken, Powery, and Rottman. See also Eric Weiner, "Where
    Heaven and Earth Come Closer," *New York Times*, March 9,
    2012, https://www.nytimes.com/2012/03/11/travel/thin-places-
    where-we-are-jolted-out-of-old-ways-of-seeing-the-world.html/.

26. Sancken, Powery, and Rottman, *Getting to God*.

27. Sancken, Powery, and Rottman.

28. Weiner, "Where Heaven and Earth."

29. Sancken, Powery, and Rottman, *Getting to God*.

30. Rev. Dr. Brian Maguire, email exchange, "Longing for the
    Transcendent?," with Joni Sancken and pastoral staff at Fairmont
    Presbyterian Church, Kettering, Ohio, April 27, 2020. Used with
    permission. See also Sancken, Powery, and Rottman, *Getting
    to God*.

31. Westermann, *Blessing*, 103–4.

32. Unattributed benediction, *Voices Together* (Harrisonburg, VA:
    MennoMedia, 2020), 1066.

33. Kate Bowler, "A Blessing for Keeping for Your Heart Soft When
    Everything Has Broken," February 22, 2022, https://katebowler
    .com/blessings/a-blessing-for-keeping-your-heart-soft-when-
    everything-is-broken/.

34. O'Donohue, *To Bless the Space*, 169.

35. Sarah McCammon, "For Kids Who Survived Tornados, Santa
    Comes 'a Little Bit Differently' This Year," NPR, December
    23, 2021, https://www.npr.org/2021/12/23/1066809237/

for-kids-who-survived-tornadoes-santa-comes-a-little-bit-differently-this-year.

36. McCammon.

37. Kaethe Weingarten, *Common Shock: Witnessing Violence Every Day* (New York: New American Library, 2003), 4.

38. Weingarten, 6.

39. Ed Prideaux, "How to Heal the 'Mass Trauma' of COVID-19," BBC, February 3, 2021, https://www.bbc.com/future/article/20210203-after-the-covid-19-pandemic-how-will-we-heal/.

40. Emily Hernandez, "Here's How to Help Uvalde Shooting Victims, Survivors and Their Families," *Texas Tribune*, May 25, 2022, https://www.texastribune.org/2022/05/25/uvalde-shooting-how-to-help/.

The Author

Joni S. Sancken is professor of homiletics at United Theological Seminary in Dayton, Ohio. Her approach to preaching is theological and interdisciplinary. She is the author of *Stumbling Over the Cross: Preaching the Cross and Resurrection Today* (Cascade, 2016) and *Words That Heal: Preaching Hope to Wounded Souls* (Abingdon Press, 2019). Joni is an ordained pastor in Mennonite Church USA and completed two levels of training with STAR (Strategies for Trauma Awareness and Resilience) through the Center for Justice and Peacebuilding at Eastern Mennonite University in 2017 and 2021. She lives in Oakwood, Ohio, with her pastor husband Steve Schumm and children Maggie and Theodore.